Joseph Kearney Foran

An Essay on Obligations

For lawyers, students and laymen

Joseph Kearney Foran

An Essay on Obligations
For lawyers, students and laymen

ISBN/EAN: 9783337233495

Printed in Europe, USA, Canada, Australia, Japan

Cover: Foto ©Suzi / pixelio.de

More available books at **www.hansebooks.com**

AN ESSAY ON

OBLIGATIONS;

FOR

LAWYERS, STUDENTS AND LAYMEN.

BY

JOSEPH K. FORAN, LL.B.

TORONTO:
CARSWELL & CO., LAW PUBLISHERS.
1886.

Entered according to Act of Parliament of the Dominion of Canada, in the year of our Lord, 1896, by CARSWELL & Co., in the office of the Minister of Agriculture.

PRINTED BY
MOORE & CO., LAW PRINTERS,
20 ADELAIDE ST. EAST,
TORONTO.

To

FRANÇOIS LANGELIER, ESQ., LL.D., M.P.,

Professor of Civil Law,

—AT—

LAVAL UNIVERSITY, QUEBEC,

AS

A TOKEN OF ESTEEM AND GRATITUDE,—ESTEEM FOR HIS HIGH
ABILITIES, DEEP RESEARCH, AND BROAD LEGAL
KNOWLEDGE; GRATITUDE FOR MANY
FAVOURS AND KINDNESSES
IN THE PAST,

THIS ESSAY IS DEDICATED

BY

His Former Pupil and Constant Friend and Admirer,

THE AUTHOR.

Green Park,
    Aylmer, Que.
    1st May, 1886.

AN ESSAY ON OBLIGATIONS.

BY

JOSEPH K. FORAN, LL.B.

PREFACE.

THE reader will find at the bottom of each page the name of the author, and the portion of the work from which the matter in the text has been translated. I say *translated* and not *quoted*; because all the works upon the Civil Laws of Lower Canada are either French or Latin. The old and modern authorities upon the Laws of France, the Code Napolèon, and consequently upon our own Code, have written in the French language, while the very first principles of those laws were given in the works of the ancient Roman jurists in the Latin language.

As it is sometimes impossible, even with circumlocution, to render in one language the exact expression of the other, whenever I find that my English falls short of the original, I give, instead of only the name of the author and the page of his book, the full French or Latin text. Thus there can be no mistake.

Also, at the foot of the page, containing any article of our Code, will be found the number of that article. I do not deem it necessary to reproduce each article in full; whenever I find it expedient to make use of any article, or portion of an article, I give it between quotation marks. I likewise indicate that which is new law. Therefore, in the text, any words found between quotation marks, are taken from the Civil Code of Lower Canada. At the bottom of the page will be found the number of the article. At the end of each paragraph is a small letter indicating the authority, at the foot of the page, from whom it has been translated. Any portions of the work not so indicated or otherwise marked out, are my own.

The names of the authorities being given in abbreviations, it might be well to here mention some of their names in full.

On Roman Law:—Justinian; Ulpien; Paul; Domat; Maynz; Ortolan; Demangeat; The Institutes; The Novels; etc.

On Old French Law.—Pardessus; Furgole; Auzanet; Dumoulin; Pothier; etc.

On Modern French Law :—Mourlon; Valette; Demolombe; Aubry and Rau; Marcadé; Duranton;

Duverger ; Laurent ; Merlin ; Lahaye-Waldeck-Rousseau ; etc.

The Code Napolèon, and Civil Code of Lower Canada.

In the first chapter I explain why and for whom this small work has been written; in the second chapter I give a synopsis of the whole *Code*, or rather, the *plan* of the Code; in the third chapter will be found a *map* of " Obligations." Consequently the Essay commences to explain the " Title of Obligations," properly speaking, only with the fourth chapter. Still these three first chapters are very necessary, above all for law-students and laymen.

Without further preface, let us take a rapid survey of this, the most important part of the Civil Laws ! Trusting that the importance of the subject, the utility of the information imparted and the necessity, daily augmenting, that each and all the citizens of Canada should know something of the law, may, to a certain extent, compensate for the poverty of the style and the many little shortcomings in the workmanship of this Essay, I give it to the public, as the fruits of considerable study and the result of long reflection.

J. K. F.

TABLE OF CONTENTS.

	PAGE.
PREFACE—	
CHAPTER I.—Introductory	1
CHAPTER II.—Plan of the Civil Code	10
CHAPTER III.—Map of Obligations	18
CHAPTER IV.—Obligations	19
SEC. I.—Contracts	20
SEC. II.—Causes of nullity	22
SEC. III.—Interpretation	28
SEC. IV.—Effect of Contracts	31
SEC. V.— " with third parties	33
SEC. VI.—Avoidance	35
CHAPTER V.—Quasi-Contracts	38
SEC. I.—Negotiorum-gestio	39
SEC. II.—Reception of thing not due	42
CHAPTER VI.—Offences and Quasi-offences	45
CHAPTER VII.—Obligations from law solely	50
CHAPTER VIII.—Object of Obligations	52
CHAPTER IX.—Effect of Obligations	54
SEC. I.—General Provisions	54
SEC. II.—Defaults	56
SEC. III.—Damages	57
CHAPTER X.—Kinds of Obligations	61
SEC. I.—Conditional Obligations	61
SEC. II.—Obligations with a term	68
SEC. III.—Alternative Obligations	70
SEC. IV.—Joint and several Obligations	72
S.-S. I.—Joint and several Creditors	72
S.-S. II.—Joint and several Debtors	74
SEC. V.—Divisible and Indivisible Obligations	87
SEC. VI.—Obligations with penal clause	94

	PAGE.
CHAPTER XI.—Extinction of Obligations	100
SEC. I.—General Provisions..	100
SEC. II.—Payment	102
S.-S. I.—General Provisions	102
S.-S. II.—Subrogation	109
S.-S. III.—Imputation	115
S.-S. IV.—Tender and Deposit	117
SEC. III.—Novation	120
SEC. IV.—Release	127
SEC. V.—Compensation	130
SEC. VI.—Confusion	135
SEC. VII.—Performance impossible	137
CHAPTER XII.—On Proof	140
CHAPTER XIII.—Synopsis of Obligations..	145
CHAPTER XIV.—Conclusion	152

CHAPTER I.

INTRODUCTORY.

M. Siffrein, in his preface to the works of Pothier, says: "We can never know the Code so long as we only study the Code. Such was the remarkable maxim proclaimed from the tribune by the deep and wise *Portalis*, at the memorable epoch of the restoration of French laws. It is, in truth, in the great body of Roman law; it is, more especially, in the works of those famous jurists, whom France so honours, that we must seek the knowledge of the true principles. Those works, stamped with the seal of equity, trace to the Roman lawgivers those eternal rules which reason suggests to all good men and inspires them with the desire to have them applied in the case of the feeble and the oppressed even as in their own cases. Pothier had recourse to the text of the *Institutes*; he procured aid from the commentaries of *Vinnius*, and thus prepared to go drink at the very fountain head of the law."

When reading the above remarks I reflected upon their truth and the idea flashed across my mind, that, in order to properly understand our laws, we need to read something more than the Civil Code. I fancied at once an objection that many might make, by stating that they could not read French. This I answer by translating the works of those French commentators into English. Again, the reader may say that he has not time to read all the endless authorities. There have been several thousand pages written upon the question of "Obligations" alone. Well, then, I overcome that difficulty for him by condensing those numberless pages into the space of a couple of hundred. Here you have, in English, a compendium of those works which are most usually quoted. It is in order to convey an idea of the real beauties and harmonies of the study of the law, while at the same time offering an easy method of studying and retaining the all important laws of obligations, that I have compiled, arranged and now present this essay.

Law, says Blackstone, is a rule of action prescribed by a superior power.

Law, says Story, in one of his introductory chapters, is the offspring of God and like Him is everywhere. Deep in the nature of things lie her fountains, and their outflowings gladden all existence. From her is the music of the universe. Before all, in all, above all, subject only to the Infinite One, she reigns over matter and mind alike.

Indeed, continues Story, the fountains of law are all one, universal, united, unchanging spring, issuing forth from the bosom of the Deity. With Him they are ever present; in Him they are ever following; like Him they are ever *one*; like Him, moreover, they are multiform in manifestation; and like Him they bless wherever they are. *Law*, in the broadest acceptation of the term, is the order of the universe, and it has as many narrower meanings as there are subjects to which our minds apply the word.

We read the truth, pervading every system of jurisprudence, that, whenever a matter comes before the courts it is really a call for a new enunciation of legal doctrines; and that from the past we only can gather a few rules to guide us in the future. We learn that both the olden light and the new point to the way of *principle* for the settlement of new cases where particular *precedents* fail.

"Very poetic all this!" The exclamation has already been made and made very sarcastically. But we must remember that there is poetry in law. The botanist, walking along the highway, perceives a small plant; at once his trained eye has detected the species and his mind, at a flash, suggests the family. Meanwhile his companion may not perceive the plant at all, or if he does notice it, he only knows that it has such or such a colour. Again the astronomer gazes upon the heavens, he sees more than a mere canopy of stars in that vast empyrean. For him the earth stands forth a suspended ball, taking its place as one of the planets and like them pursuing its appointed path, the arbiter of times and seasons. Beyond our planetary system, extended by the discovery of Neptune, to three thousand millions of miles from the sun and throughout the expanse of the universe, the telescope exhibts to him new suns and systems of worlds, infinite in number and variety. As you progress you behold on all sides wonders and changes—in the history of the ages—the progress of society—in the improvements and inventions of the times. So must you notice the same in the rise, progress and changes of the laws, which ever and always keep pace with the march of humanity and, like each of the other sciences, irresistibly draw our attention to the wonderful workings of God and the majesty and genius of His creature man.

Not only is there poetry in the real study of the law, but history, science, literature, all go hand-in-hand with the law. There being a certain harmony in the law, even as in the systems of the universe, it is well to point it out at times, and it is always dangerous to disturb it. In this essay I have attempted to indicate the progress of the principles that rule us to-day, and to convey to the reader an idea, concise and exact, of our laws of obligations, without clashing with the Civil Code or any of the authorities.

Mourlon, in the preface to his second volume on the Civil Code, says :—I have followed the order of the Code, as to the titles and sections ; but I have wandered from the order of the articles whenever it appeared to me to be defective. Sometimes, indeed, the dispositions of a section are like a heap of rules without any connection or reference to each other, which renders the study of the text both laborious and difficult ; for, in order to grasp the proper meaning of many of them, it is necessary to unite considerable application to a great deal of discernment. This want of order is the cause that, at the very commencement of their careers, many students, who have no guide, are too often discouraged and bring to their work minds that are already tired and lazy. When the memory is loaded and the judgment embarrassed with a confusion of ill-regulated decisions, it is difficult to form for oneself a clear and exact system and to arrange in the mind that which is so disarranged in the book. I have not sought to be elegant in style. Before all, I wished to be clear, logical and to make each principle exact, also to render the study of the law so easy that the most rebellious minds may attempt it with encouragement and pleasure.

To a certain extent I may, here, reproduce those words of Mourlon and apply them to this little essay.

For three classes have these pages been composed. Firstly, for the lawyers of the Province of Quebec; Secondly, for the law students; and Thirdly, for the laymen, merchants, traders, farmers, &c., whether in the Province of Quebec or in the Province of Ontario.

A word to each of the three categories of my readers, before entering upon the study!

Firstly.—The lawyers of the Province of Quebec may herein find the compendium of those works from which our principles of Civil Law are derived. Again these pages with their lists of authorities may serve as an index to the larger volumes from which these extracts have been taken. In so much this essay may be of use to both the English and French speaking members of the Bar. For them no further explanation or introduction is necessary; they know the value of a legal dictionary or a legal index, just as the merchant knows the value of a ready-reckoner.

Secondly.—To the law-students. In the next chapter you will find a synopsis or plan of the whole Code, so arranged that, by once reading it, even the dullest aspirant must remember its contents. Without method or system the study of the law is an endless labour, tiresome and profitless; but once a plan is drawn out, a method adopted, there is no study so easy and so pleasant. Let a man visit the catacombs without a light and a guide and what is the result? Without the light he must stumble, become entangled, fall and perhaps injure himself; without the guide he will certainly get lost. It is so in the endless labyrinth and winding corridors of the law.

In the third chapter you will find a *map* or synopsis of the "Title of Obligations." Stamp that one page upon your memory and you will never forget the fundamental laws of obligations. No matter when an examination may be called you will be ready. At the end I give another synopsis fuller and minuter. But it is necessary to read over the whole essay in order to derive much benefit from it. Let the student study well *my system of studying obligations* and he can then apply it to the study of all the other parts of the Civil Code.

Thirdly.—To the laymen, (merchants, farmers, men of all trades and professions outside the profession of the law). Especially, almost, for your benefit have I compiled and composed these pages. It is a saying, very common, if not very exact, that "every one is supposed to know the law." How far the maxim is true will be explained hereafter, but for the present let us remember that, whether it be the case or not that every one is supposed to know the law, it is certainly of great use to each one to have an idea, clear and correct, of the general dispositions of the laws that govern him and regulate his rights and wrongs. In two cases, more especially, do you find the want of that general knowledge and do you fully appreciate its value. Let us examine both cases.

Firstly.—When you deem yourself injured and are doubtful whether you have a legal right to *an action at law* or not.

Secondly.—Whenever a neighbour or other person sues you, or threatens to, or actually does summon you before the courts. If he has a right to *an action at law* against you, it is worse than useless for you to defend your case. In fact it would be a great loss to you were you to take up the contest. On the other hand, if he has *no* right to such *action at law*, it behooves you to join issue with him.

Now, when have you and when have you not a right to an *action at law*? I will, here, answer the question in a general manner and you may conclude therefrom the benefit it will be to you to read on and discover, in these few pages, the details of that general answer. In other words, you will find the law made clear, simple and exact.

There are two things necessary, both of which must have had existence, before an action at law may be had. Firstly, an *obligation;* and secondly, the *violation* of that obligation. The latter supposes the former, but the former does not necessarily suppose the existence of the latter. An obligation may have existed and become extinguished, and yet neither of the parties have a right to an action before the courts. By a simple example I will illustrate the idea I wish to convey and, at the same time, demonstrate the necessity of a clear knowledge of obligations.

Jones and Smith are neighbours. They have had no communication, in any way, with each other; there has never been nor is there now any obligation existing between them. Neither then has a right to an *action* against the other. But Jones offers Smith $100 for his black horse and Smith accepts the offer. At once two obligations arise (springing from the contract of sale). Jones is obliged to pay the $100, while Smith is obliged to give over to Jones the possession of the black horse. Smith transfers the horse, his obligation is extinguished, (by means of payment); but Jones refuses or neglects to pay the $100. At once he violates his obligation, and upon that *violation* is founded an *action* at law in favour of Smith. The fact of the obligation existing did not give a right to that action; it was the existence of the obligation coupled with the violation of it.

I hear you say that you knew all that before, without my writing it down for your benefit. It is the simplicity of the illustration that makes you imagine that you knew it before. Now do you know *when* an obligation exists?—what the sources of obligations are?—how many kinds of obligations may arise?—how many ways, and by what means an obligation may be extinguished? You don't answer. Well, if by a series of simple examples, I answer all these questions for you and so illustrate them that you cannot be mistaken in the future, I expect to hear you say, when you have laid aside this little work, that *you knew all that before.* If so I shall be satisfied, as in that remark I shall hear the best and most favourable comment I could desire for upon my essay.

The following chapter is written, principally, for law-students, but the lawyer and layman may both find in it some little information that might be of use to them.

CHAPTER II.

PLAN OF THE CIVIL CODE.

The late Mr. Justice McCord, of Quebec, in his preface to the 1867 edition of the Civil Code of Lower Canada, remarks : " The Commissioners presented in all eight Reports on the Civil Code. The first Report, dated 12th October, 1861, contained the draft of the title OF OBLIGATIONS, which, because of its importance, as being the basis of the greater portion of the whole Code, it had been decided to commence with. For the same reason, this title was, even more than any of the others, the subject of long and careful examination and discussion." Again referring to the authorities quoted under each article of the Civil Code, the same writer says : " It must not be supposed that all these authorities are in support of the text ; some are directly opposed to the articles above them. As already stated, they are the authorities consulted by the Commissioners, and nothing more." We see from this to what a small degree we can depend upon the authorities found mentioned in the Code. It is necessary to seek out authorities for ourselves.

In another place, in the same preface, Mr. Justice McCord remarks: "These special references are by no means intended to restrict the reading of the Code to the articles enumerated, or to enable any class of persons to dispense with a knowledge of the other portions of the work. It is assumed that, *even outside of Lower Canada*, every literate man in the Dominion ought to avail himself of the means afforded him by our Quebec Code, to obtain a general knowledge of the laws of the oldest of the Confederate Provinces." In terminating the same preface the learned judge says: "The English speaking residents of Lower Canada may now enjoy the satisfaction of at least possessing in their own language the laws by which they are governed, and the Province of Quebec will bring with her into the Confederation a system of laws of which she may be justly proud: a system mainly founded on the steadfast, time-honoured and equitable principles of the civil laws, and which not only merits admiration and respect, but presents a worthy model for legislation elsewhere."

From these remarks I naturally conclude that the authorities quoted under the articles of our Code are not all exact and that many contradict the Code. I may here state that our Code is very deficient in definitions. I also conclude that before the Code the English speaking residents of the Province of Quebec had no statement of the laws in their own language. And since the Code few, if any, have written in English upon those laws. With the exception of a "carefully written pamphlet by Thomas Ritchie, Esq., containing observations upon the title *Of Obligations,*" nothing has appeared upon this the most important and most fundamental part of the Code. Finally, I infer from that preface, that a knowledge of those principles and laws is required outside the Province of Quebec as well as within its limits.

I proposed giving, in this chapter, a *plan* of the Code. By plan I do not mean a synopsis of the whole work and its contents. That would require several hundred pages. It is merely an indication of the line of reasoning followed, very naturally, by the codifiers in disposing and arranging the different titles and sections. If the student will pay special attention to the next couple of pages he may find therein a system or plan which, if once grasped and understood, will always be a guide and an aid in remembering the contents of the Code.

Firstly.—It is well to know who is and who is not a British subject, for the law suffers many exceptions in the case of aliens. Therefore does the Code begin the First Book with the explanation of who are British subjects and upon civil rights, how gained, how lost. But the Code does not define an *alien.* In fact it gives very few definitions. We shall have to supply them. An alien is a foreigner. The registration of acts of civil status, that is birth, death, marriage, &c., naturally follow, and the question of domicile and that of absentees come next in order. The whole of the First Book refers to *persons.* In the

Second Book we read of *things*. Just reflect for a moment upon the logical order of these books.

The laws are intended to define the rights of persons. Then first of all persons must exist. The question of *marriage* is consequently treated of at the very outset. The laws regulating *separation from bed and board* follow very naturally. We then commence the life of a person springing from that marriage and follow it through all its phases.

Before its birth—the question of *filiation*. Then, as soon as born, comes the question of *paternal authority*. For the first years of its life it is a minor. Then we have the laws regulating *minority* and its accidents, *tutorship* and *emancipation*. Tutorship being the guardianship of the minor and emancipation being his delivery, by extraordinary means, from the bondage of minority. Then follows the title of *majority* with its accidents of *interdiction*, *curatorship* and *judicial advisers*.

Now we have followed the British subject from birth, through all the stages, up to majority, or legal manhood. That ends the question of persons as individuals. Now there are other legal persons called *corporations*. A corporation is a body composed of one or many individuals, forming one legal being, and being perpetual at least in theory. With corporations ends the First Book.

Now that you have *persons* the next requisite, to establish those rights, is an object, or, in other words, *things*. The Second Book, then, distinguished things into moveable and immoveable. Having *persons* and *things*, you next require to know what connection exists between them. The first is *ownership*. When the Code disposes of the laws regulating the *ownership* of a *thing* by a *person*, it passes on to the other minor connections that may exist. Of these we first meet with *usufruct*, then *use* and *habitation*. Besides these direct claims of persons to things there are other lesser rights which arise in the forms of *servitudes* and *emphyteusis*.

So far we have 1st, persons; 2nd, things; 3rd, direct and indirect connections between the two. The question that now naturally suggests itself to the legal mind is: How may *persons* acquire those rights upon *things?* There are several ways, and the Code takes them up in their logical order. The Second Book ends with those claims of persons on things, and the Third Book opens with the different modes of the *acquisition of property*.

The first means, then, of acquiring property is by *successions*. That important title of the Code comprises 158 articles. The next important means of acquiring property is by *gifts inter vivos* and by *will*. These, including *substitutions*, take up 228 articles.

Up to this we have 1st, persons; 2nd, things; 3rd, connection between persons and things; and 4th, acquisition of property. So far the law treats of silent or inactive rights. Now it behooves us to examine into active rights, that is those claims of persons on persons, or persons on things put into action or motion by means of *actions at law*. As I before explained, no action at law can exist until there has first been an *obligation*, and then the *violation* of that obligation. Coming now to the assertion of rights or the defence of them before the tribunals, we must first know what an obligation is when it exists, from what it may arise, how many forms it may assume, and how it dies out.

Consequently the next title of the Code is that *of obligations*. It is with this we shall have to deal in the present work. The law having defined those obligations goes on to explain in detail the different contracts from which they may arise, and the many modifications to which these contracts are subject. Therefore we find the fourth title commencing with *marriage covenants*. This title includes the laws of *dower*. Then we have the different actions that may take place between persons with regard to things. *Sale, lease and hire, mandate, loan, deposit, partnership, liferents, transaction, gaming contracts and bets, suretyship, privileges and hypothecs, registration of real rights,* and finally *prescription*.

The Fourth Book is on Commercial Law, Bills of Exchange, Notes, Cheques, Merchant Shipping, Affreightment, Carriage of Passsengers, Insurance, Bottomry and Respondentia.

Behold now the whole Code revolving around the title of obligations. As the rays to a burning focus, all the titles and sections converge towards obligations on the one hand, while in equal lines do they diverge therefrom on the other. It is like the central planet of a system, supporting all the others while keeping them at regular distances. You have now the great arch of the civil law spanning the history of a British subject and his rights, from the marriage of his parents, on through his minority, then majority, the acquisition of his rights, the changes they may be subjected to, until he reaches their final extinction or renewal in prescription. And of that arch the key-stone is the title of obligations. Take away that key-stone, and the whole fabric comes down with a crash.

In order then to remember the plan of the Code, you have only to commence at your birth, or rather the marriage of your parents, and follow your own career up to the age of twenty-one. Then consider that any claim you may have to a thing (moveable or immoveable) arises from either ownership or servitude, and that in order to have such claim you must have got it either by succession, gift, or will. Finally that any disturbance of that claim must lead you to the consideration of the title of obligations, and that the rest of the Code is but the development of the principles laid down in that title.

So far, strictly speaking, I might call all my remarks introductory; and truly they are more or less so. It may seem quite out of proportion to the bulk of the essay to have so many pages of introduction. But I deemed them necessary, and moreover, if you like, you may consider them part of the essay itself.

I wish to draw special attention to the next chapter, which is nothing other than a map of the title *Of Obligations*. It will serve as a guide in following me through the different parts of the essay. Also it will be of use to stamp upon the student's mind the plan of this very important portion of the Code.

You will see by this plan that I will first define Obligations—the Code does not do so. Then I will give the *sources* of Obligations with the omitted definitions. Then the *effects* of Obligations. Then the different *kinds* of Obligations; and lastly, the *extinction* of Obligations. At the close the reader will find a minute and detailed synopsis, and a chapter referring to *proof* of Obligations.

There are 275 articles under the title of Obligations; of these 54 treat of *proof* and *testimony*.

It is as well to remark here that several of the articles of the Civil Code (which has been twenty years in force) have been changed, more or less, by statutory legislation. As I do not pretend to follow the Code more than the authorities, but merely purpose confining myself to the exposition of the *general principles* of Obligations, I cannot point out these different changes. It would form subject for a very useful work by itself. This essay is more for students and laymen than for members of the legal profession.

CHAPTER III.

MAP OF OBLIGATIONS.

I. Sources of Obligations.
- 1st. Contracts.
  - 1st. Marriage Covenants.
  - 2nd. Sale.
  - 3rd. Lease and Hire.
  - 4th. Mandate.
  - 5th. Loan.
  - 6th. Deposit.
  - 7th. Partnership.
  - 8th. Life Rents.
  - 9th. Transaction.
  - 10th. Bets—Gaming Debts.
  - 11th. Suretyship.
  - 12th Privileges and Hypothecs.
  - 13th. Prescription.
- 2nd. Quasi-Contracts.
  - 1st. Negotiorum gestio.
  - 2nd. Reception of a thing not due.
- 3rd. Offences.
- 4th. Quasi-Offences.
- 5th. Result of the Law.

II. Effects of Obligations.
- 1st. Default.
- 2nd. Damages resulting therefrom.

III. Kinds of Obligations.
- 1st. Conditional.
- 2nd. With a Term.
- 3rd. Alternative.
- 4th. Joint and Several.
  - 1st. Joint and Several Creditors.
  - 2nd. Joint and Several Debtors.
- 5th. Divisible and Indivisible.
- 6th. With a Penal Clause.

IV. Ordinary means of Extinction of Obligations.
- 1st. Payment.
  - 1st. In General.
  - 2nd. With Subrogation.
  - 3rd. Imputation of Payment.
  - 4th. Tender and Deposit.
- 2nd. Novation.
- 3rd. Release.
- 4th. Compensation.
- 5th. Confusion.
- 6th. Performance becoming Impossible.

V. Extraordinary means of Extinction of Obligations.
- 1st. Judgment in Nullity.
- 2nd. Effect of Resolutive Condition.
- 3rd. Prescription.
- 4th. By Expiration of Time Limited by Law or by the Parties for its Duration.
- 5th. By Death of Creditor or Debtor in certain cases.
- 6th. By special Clauses Applicable to Particular Contracts.

CHAPTER IV.

OBLIGATIONS.

What is an Obligation ? (*a*) Our Code does not tell us, so we must seek elsewhere for a proper definition.

An Obligation is a legal tie by which one person is bound towards another to give, to do, or not to do something (*b*).

There are imperfect and perfect Obligations. The former may be styled *duty*, or what we owe to God or our neighbour, like charity, gratitude, &c. The latter are those giving the one against whom they are contracted a right to demand their execution (*c*).

A legal tie is a figure of speech, a metaphor employed to designate the means of enforcing its fulfilment (*d*).

Obligations *to give* and *to do* differ. Error of person rarely causes the nullity of an Obligation *to give*, but often causes the nullity of an Obligation *to do* something (*e*).

(*a*) Arts. 982 & 983.
(*b*) *Vinculum juris quo necessitate astringimur alicujus rei Solvendæ* Just. tit. de Oblig. L. 13 ff. de Oblig.
(*c*) Poth. Ob. N. I.
(*d*) Mourlon vol. ii. No. 1024.
(*e*) *Idem*.

Three conditions are "essential to an Obligation that it should have a cause from which it arises, persons between whom it exists and an object" (*a*).

"Obligations arise from contracts, quasi-contracts, offences, quasi-offences and from the operation of the law solely" (*b*).

Section I.—*Contracts.*

A contract is not defined in the Code (*c*). It will be remarked, as we proceed, how very few legal definitions the Code supplies. What is a contract?

Contract is a convention whereby two parties reciprocally, or one of them only promises and binds himself to give, to do, or not to do something (*d*).

It has also been defined as the agreement of two or more persons upon the same object (*e*).

The species of convention known as a contract is that which has for its object the formation of some engagement (*f*).

A convention or contract has again been styled the agreement of two wills to produce a legal effect. That legal effect may be either the creation of one or more

(*a*) Art. 982.
(*b*) Art. 983.
(*c*) Art. 984.
(*d*) Poth. ob. 3.
(*e*) *Duorum vel plurium in idem placitum consensus.*
(*f*) Poth. ob. 3.

Obligations, or the extinction or modification of an existing Obligation, or else, (what did not exist in the days of Pothier) a changement of property (*a*).

A contract is a convention by which one or many persons (oblige themselves) bind themselves towards one or many others to give, to do, or not to do something (*b*).

"There are four requisites to the validity of a contract: parties legally capable of contracting; their consent legally given; something which forms the object of the contract; a lawful cause or consideration" (*c*).

"Upon each of these four requisites let us say a word. Those incapable of contracting are minors; interdicted persons; married women in certain cases; those who for reason of relationship are forbidden by the law; persons insane or suffering from a temporary derangement of intellect arising from illness or other cause" (*d*). "Consent may be either express or implied." "A contract without a consideration or with an unlawful consideration has no effect." "The consideration is unlawful when it is prohibited by law, or is contrary to good morals, or public order."

It would be tedious and unnecessary to enter into the technical details of the different kinds of contracts. There are contracts called *synallagmatiques*

(*a*) Mour. vol. ii. No. 1026.
(*b*) C. N. 1101.
(*c*) Art. 984.
(*d*) Arts. 985 to 991.

and *unilateráux* by the French authors. The sale of a house is an example of the former; the deposit of a sum is an example of the latter. There are seven or eight other divisions made upon which the authorities do not all agree.

There is an old maxim of Roman law which divides the contracts into four species; but these distinctions would only confuse us now without materially aiding in the accomplishment of our object (a).

In Roman law they recognized only four contracts that took effect by mere consent : sale, lease, partnership and mandate. Hence their maxim *solus consensus non obligat*. But what was the exception with them has become the rule with us, and the Code only recognizes five solemn contracts: gifts, hypothecs, adoption, and the two marriage contracts. Thus the rule with us the contrary of Roman law *solus consensus obligat* (b).

The above applies to the French Code of Napoleon.

Section II.—*Causes of Nullity.*

" Error, fraud, violence or fear, and lesion are causes of nullity in contracts; subject to the limitations and rules contained in this Code " (c). " Error

(a) *Do ut des, Facio ut facies, Facio ut des, Do ut facies.*
(b) Mour. vol. ii. No. 1035.
(c) Art. 991.

is a cause of nullity only when it occurs in the nature of the contract itself, or in the substance of the thing which is the object of the contract, or in something which is a principal consideration for making it. (*a*)."

Error is a belief at variance with truth and in some cases it is a cause of absolute nullity, and in other cases it merely renders the contract annulable.

The following *resumé* will explain when error is a cause of nullity, when it renders the contract annulable, and when it has no effect upon the validity of the contract. An example then of one or two cases will suffice to suggest to the reader examples of all the others.

Error on { 1st. The nature of the convention. 2nd. The object of the convention. } Contract is *null*.

Error on { 1st. The substance of the object. 2nd. The person when the identity of the person has an effect on the contract. } Contract is *annulable*.

Error on { 1st. The unsubstantial qualities. 2nd. The motive of the contract. 3rd. The person, when the consideration of the person is of no effect in the contract. } Contract is *good*. (*b*).

(*a*) Art. 992.
(*b*) Mour. vol. ii. No. 1048.

I will now explain by a short example the second case in each of the above and the reader can occupy his mind with the invention of examples for the other cases.

No. 2 in the first batch says, that "Error on the object of the convention renders the contract null." I intend to sell Peter my house A. By some error or mistake he thinks it is my house B. that I am selling him. The contract is *null*. Let us see No. 2, in the second batch. "Error with regard to the person, when the identity of the person has an effect on the contract." I hire, or intend to hire A., who is a famous painter, to do a piece of work; by some error it is B., a painter of less note who undertakes the work. The contract is open to be *annulled* if I like. Now No. 2 in the third batch. "Error in the motive of the the contract does not disturb it." I thought my horse had been burned in a stable that was destroyed by fire. My motive is to replace my horse by another, and I consequently buy another. After I have bought the new horse I find out that my own old horse escaped the fire. My error of motive does not change the contract. It remains intact (*a*).

Here arises the question whether a contract is null in consequence of an *error in law*. In other words, is the old maxim true, that no person is supposed to ignore the law? *Nemo censetur ignorare legem*. In criminal law this maxim is true. Otherwise crimes

(*a*) *Idem* No. 1046.

might be committed and persons hide themselves under the cloak of their ignorance. But in civil law it cannot stand. And why? Firstly, because it is written no place in law, and secondly, because it would be unjust and deprive the very persons, for whose protection the law is established, of its benefits, viz., the ignorant and illiterate (*a*).

"Fraud is a cause of nullity when the artifices practised by one party or with his knowledge, are such that the other party would not have contracted without them. It is never presumed and must be proved" (*b*).

Fraud (dol) is any species of artifice (trickery) made use of by one person to cheat (deceive) another (*c*).

Only the fraud that gave rise to the contract can be a cause of its nullity. All other frauds are merely causes for damages (*d*).

"Violence or fear is a cause of nullity, whether practised or produced by the party for whose benefit the contract is made, or by any other person" (*e*).

The fear must be reasonable and the violence must be serious. Age, sex, character, &c., must be taken into consideration. Mere reverential fear of a father

(*a*) *Idem* No. 1048, sec. 2.
(*b*) Art. 993.
(*c*) Poth. Ob. 28, also L. I. sec. 1, ff. *de dol.*
(*d*) Poth. Ob. 31.
(*e*) Art. 994.

or other, without violence or threats is not sufficient to annul a contract (*a*).

In any case the will, even restrained, *is still* THE WILL, say the ancients (*b*). But when violence is used neither by civil nor by natural law is the contract valid (*c*).

When a third party causes the violence Grotius thinks that it is from civil law alone the remedy comes, but Pufendorf and Barbeyrac think it comes from both civil and natural law. The fear must be one of a great evil, *metu majoris mali*, otherwise it does not render the contract null. • If you shake a stick at me and say you will hit me unless I sign a deed of sale, that would not be violence sufficient to produce a fear so intense that I would yield against my will.

If I am drowning and you will pull me out on condition I give you an enormous sum, the contract is not *annulable* but merely *reducible*. An evil feared to my property must be *considerable* and *actually present*. For example, a man threatening to burn my house and actually prepared to do so.

"Lesion is a cause of nullity only in certain cases, and with respect to certain persons, as explained in this section" (*d*).

Pothier says *majors* may demand restitution for *lésion énorme* (excessive lesion); but *minors* can demand

---

(*a*) Arts. 994 to 1000.
(*b*) *Voluntas coacta est voluntas.* Gloss, L. 21, sec. 5.
(*c*) Poth. Ob. 22, *et Gros de jure bell. lib.* 2, cap. 11, n. 7.
d) Art. 1001.

it in all cases (*a*). But modern commentators upon the Code Napoleòn state that only in two cases, that of *sale* and that of *division*, and only with regard to *minors* does a contract become null from the effects of lesion (*b*).

"A minor who is a banker, trader or mechanic, is not relievable for cause of lesion from contracts made for the purposes of his business or trade" (*c*).

The next two articles of our Code are new law and I give them here in full.

"A minor is not relievable from the stipulations contained in his marriage contract, when they have been made with the consent and assistance of those whose consent is required for the validity of his marriage" (*d*). The next is:

"When all the formalities required with respect to minors or interdicted persons for the alienation of immoveable property, or the partition of a succession, have been observed, such contracts, and acts have the same force and effect as if they had been executed by persons of the age of majority and free from interdiction" (*e*).

Despite the opinion of Pothier as to *majors* being relieved in cases of excessive lesion, our Code contains an article of new law to the contrary.

(*a*) Poth. Ob. 40.
(*b*) Art. 1118, C. N. *et* Mourlon, vol. ii. No. 1061.
(*c*) Art. 1005.
(*d*) Art. 1006.
(*e*) Art. 1010.

"Persons of the age of majority are not entitled to relief from their contracts for cause of lesion only"(a).

Section III.—*Interpretation of Contracts.*

Common intention rather than literal meaning of the words must determine a doubtful contract. If two meanings may be had, it is to be understood in that in which it has most effect. Usage of the country has a great deal to do with determining a doubt. In doubtful cases the clause is interpreted against the one stipulating (b). Let us illustrate by a few examples.

You hold a lease of two rooms in my house. I renew your lease at the year's end. In drawing out the renewal I say that I lease you *my house*, for so much, for so many years, &c. The common intention is the lease of the two rooms, therefore the renewal does not affect the house (c).

Another example: It is agreed between Peter and Paul that Paul may have a right of passage over his property. Whose property? Evidently over Peter's;

(a) 1012.
(b) Arts. 1013 to 1022.
(c) Poth. Ob. 91. (*et*) *In conventionibus contrahentium voluntatem potius quam verba spectari placuit.* L. 219. *ff. de verb. signif.*

for Paul requires no written agreement or other permit to pass over his own property (*a*).

Another example: I lease you a house for nine years at $300. There is no more said in the contract. Is that to be $300 per year or else $300 for the nine years? It is to be $300 *for each year*, because annual payment is of the nature of lease, unless you prove that the place is only worth $30 or $40 *per* year. Then it would be for the nine. If the contract contains the word *repairs*—it means the *necessary repairs*; for a lessee is only held to such (*b*).

In sale, if no guarantee from eviction be mentioned, it exists all the same (*c*).

A lease states that the farmer should deliver 1,000 bushels of oats yearly to the owner of the land. Where is he to deliver them? If not mentioned in the lease, it is at the farmer's house: if the owner wanted them delivered at his place it should be mentioned in the lease (*d*).

One clause is interpreted by the others—or "all the clauses of a contract are interpreted the one by the other, giving to each the meaning derived from the entire act (*e*).

If a legatee compromise with an heir, for his rights, for a certain sum, resulting from the will of the

---

(*a*) Poth. Ob. 92.
(*b*) Poth. Ob. 93.
(*c*) 1017 C. C. L. C.; 1160 C. N.; Poth. Ob. 95.
(*d*) Poth. Ob. 97.
(*e*) Art. 1018.

deceased—it does not exclude him from his claims to another legacy, made by codicil since their transaction (*a*).

In a marriage covenant it is said that all moveables of the succession that may fall to them shall enter, that is merely to obviate all doubt upon that certain point; but it does not hinder all other things entering into the community that should belong to it (*b*).

In contracts as well as in wills, a clause in the plural often divides itself into several clauses in the singular.

Example.—A. and B. are obliged to give G. $100; that is A. is obliged to give G. $50 and B. is obliged to give G. $50 (*c*).

What is at the close of a phrase generally applies to the whole phrase and not only to what immediately precedes it; provided that the close of the phrase agrees in number and gender with the rest of it (*d*).

Example.—I sell you all the hay and oats and wheat cut this year. *Cut this year* applies to hay, oats and the wheat equally. Not so if my contract said, I sell you the hay, oats and *all the wheat* cut this year (*e*).

"In cases of doubt the contract is interpreted against him who has stipulated, and in favor of him who has contracted the obligation" (*f*).

(*a*) Poth. Ob. 98.
(*b*) Poth. Ob. 100.
(*c*) Poth. Ob. 101.
(*d*) Poth. Ob. 102.
(*e*) *Pand. Justin. tit. de leg.* N. 189 *et* 190.
(*f*) Art. 1019.

This is too strict a statement. In a synalagmatical contract where both parties are debtor and creditor at once, against whom is the doubt? Against the creditor when he attempts to establish a case that he cannot clearly prove. Against the debtor when he tries to get off from a debt that is clearly proven (*a*).

Section IV.—*Effect of contracts.*

Contracts produce Obligations, and discharge or modify other contracts. They have effect only between those contracting—the obligation of a contract is not limited to what is expressed in it, but extends to all consequences thereof, legal etc. (*b*).

This is new law and requires to be given in full. " A contract for the alienation of a thing certain and determinate makes the purchaser owner of the thing by consent alone of the parties, although no delivery be made.—The foregoing rule is subject to special provisions contained in this Code concerning the transfer and registry of vessels. The safe-keeping and risk of the thing before delivery are subject to the general rules contained in the chapters *of the effect of obligations* and *of the extinction of obligations* in this title " (*c*). Creditor cannot become owner of an un-

(*a*) Mour. vol. ii. No. 1164.
(*b*) Arts. 1022 to 1028.
(*c*) Art. 1025.

certain or indeterminate thing. The next article is also new law.

"The rules contained in the two last preceding articles, apply as well to third persons as to the contracting parties, subject, in contracts for the transfer of immoveable property, to the special provisions contained in this Code for the registration of titles to the claims upon such property. But if a party oblige himself successively to two persons to deliver to each of them a thing which is purely moveable property, that one of the two who has been put in actual possession is preferred, and remains owner of the thing although his title be posterior in date ; provided, however, that his possession be in good faith " (*a*).

A principle that applies to both contracts and obligations is that "a convention has only effect with regard to the things that form the object of the convention, and only between the contracting parties themselves " (*b*).

The first part of the principle is evident ; the parties having, by will, made the contract, it cannot have effect upon other objects than those the parties had in view. So for the second part of the principle; it cannot affect third parties who have no connection with the affair.

Example.—I agree with my co-heirs that they take

(*a*) Art. 1027.

(*b*) *Animadvertendum est ne 'conventio in aliâ re facta aut cum aliâ personâ, in aliâ re, aliâve personâ, oceat,* L. 27, sec. 4, ff. de pactis:

the charge of a certain debt : my creditor is not bound by that, as he had no consent in the affair (a).

A debtor unable to pay his debts makes a compromise with three-fourths of his creditors. That will bind the other fourth who did not agree (b).

This is not an exception to the principle; for the consent of the three-fourths does not constitute the tie that binds the other fourth. It merely proves that it is the interest of the creditors to accept the compromise (c).

The right given the creditor to follow, by action, the object of a contract is not a claim upon *it*, but a mere personal claim upon the debtor to force *him* to give it up (d).

SECTION V.—*Effect of contracts with regard to third persons.*

" A party cannot, by a contract in his own name, bind anyone but himself and his heirs and legal representatives " (e). He may stipulate for the benefit of another. He is always presumed to have stipulated for himself, until the contrary is proven. A creditor may exercise a debtor's right of action when the latter refuses to do so, to the prejudice of the former.

(a) Poth. Ob. 86.
(b) Ordonance of 1673, tit. 11, arts. 5, 6, 7 et 8.
(c) Poth. Ob. 88.
(d) Poth. Ob. 151, and L. 3, ff. de Obligat. et Act.
(e) Arts. 1028 to 1032.

4

No one can stipulate for another (*a*).

These principles come to us unchanged from the days of the Romans (*b*).

I cannot bind a third party by my promise and when I promise for a third party I don't bind myself.

Example.—*Primus* says: I buy your horse for *Secundus* my mandator. *In fact Primus*, the mandatary is the one who promises and stipulates. *In law* it is *Secundus*, the mandator, who is the promising and stipulating party. So the maxim is true, that a mandatary can lawfully stipulate for his mandator, and lawfully bind him towards third parties (*c*).

The following two rules from French law regulate the questions of this section:—

1st. In general no one can bind any one except himself by agreement in his own name. 2nd. In general one can only stipulate, in his own name, for himself. How can you, in your own name, promise the act of another? The hypothesis is impossible. Pothier is clearer than the French Code on this point (*d*).

However, I can bind a third party—1st. Whenever I have a mandate from him. 2nd. Whenever the contract I undertake for him is to his great benefit (*e*).

(*a*) *Alteri stipulari nemo potest.* Ulpien.

(*b*) *Si quis velit alienum factum promittere, pœnam vel quanti ea res est, potest promettere.* Ulpien, L. 38, sec. 2, ff. d. t. Grotius *ibid.* Pufendorf. Poth. Ob. 56.

(*c*) Mour. vol. ii. No. 1065.

(*d*) Mour. vol. ii. No. 1066.

(*e*) Mour. vol. ii. No. 1067. Comp. M. Demangeat, *caurs élém, de droit romain*, t. ii. *sur le Titre De inutil stipul.*

SECTION VI.—*Avoidance of Contract and Payments made in Fraud of Creditors.*

"Creditors may in their own name impeach the acts of their debtors in fraud of their rights" (*a*). "A contract cannot be avoided unless it is made by the debtor with intent to defraud." "A gratuitous contract is supposed to be made with intent to defraud." "An onerous contract by an insolvent debtor is deemed to be with intent to defraud."

New law.—"No contract or payment can be avoided by reason of any thing contained in this section, at the suit of any individual creditor, unless such suit is brought within one year from the time of his obtaining a knowledge thereof. If the suit be by assignees or other representatives of the creditors collectively, it must be brought within a year from the time of their appointment" (*b*).

Creditors may attack all acts of their debtors made in fraud of their rights (*c*).

In order to attain this end, in Roman law, the Prætors gave the *Action Paulienne.* It is so called from the name of the Prætor who instituted it (*d*).

To have a right to this action, (in case of *actes à tirte onéreux*) the creditor must prove, 1st, prejudice

(*a*) Arts. 1032 to 1041.
(*b*) Art. 1040.
(*c*) Mour. vol. ii. No. 1186. See Insolvent Act of 1864 and the recent amendments.
(*d*) Inst. Jus. lib. iv. tit. vi. sec. 6, art. 1167 C. N.

to his interests (*eventus*); 2nd, fraud on part of the debtor (*consilium*); and 3rd, compliance of the one dealing with him. In cases of acts *à tirte gratuit*, the creditor can take action against the donors, even in good faith, and he need only prove, 1st, prejudice, and 2nd, fraud (*a*).

By the *Action Paulienne*, creditors may attack the acts by which a debtor fraudulently diminished his estate, but not acts whereby he neglected to augment it (*b*).

Creditors, anterior to an act of renunciation, may have the use of the *Action Paulienne;* but not those that come after that act, because the rights of the latter did not exist at the time of the act, and therefore no fraud could have been done them (*c*).

Those against whom the *Action Paulienne* may be used are—1st. Those who acquire under onerous title, when they are accomplices in the fraud. 2nd. Against those who acquire by gratuitous title, even though they be in good faith. 3rd. Against their universal heirs and successors (*d*).

The effect of the *Action Paulienne* is to place things

(*a*) Mour. 1176, vol. ii.; Dur. vol. x. No. 575; Marc. art. 1167; Larombière, vol. i. art. 1167, No. 26; Demol. vol. ii. No. 190.

(*b*) Mour. vol. ii. No. 1178.

(*c*) *Idem* 1181.

(*d*) *Idem* 1182, Dur. vol. x. p. 582; Val. Aubry and Rau, vol. iv. sec. 313, note 4; Marc. art. 1167; Demol. vol. ii. No. 198.

in the state in which they were previous to the act of fraud (a).

(This revocation brings the goods back to the estate; and it is only the *anterior* creditors that demand the action. Therefore, it should set aside for them the goods thus brought back.) This is a false reasoning. There are only two means of preferment, viz., privileges and hypothecs. If you give the *anterior* creditors a sole right in the benefits of the act of revocation you establish a preference that exists no place in law (b).

(a) Mour. vol. ii. No. 1183; Colmet de Santerre, vol. v. No. 82; Troplong sur privil. vol. i. Nos. 11, 14, 15.

(b) Laromb. vol. i. art. 1167; Mour. vol. ii. No. .1183; *contra*, Dur. vol. x. No. 574; Marc. art. 1167.

CHAPTER V.

QUASI-CONTRACTS.

"A person capable of contracting may, by his lawful and voluntary act, oblige himself towards another, and sometimes oblige another towards him, without the intervention of any contract between them" (*a*).

"A person incapable of contracting may, by the quasi-contract which results from the act of another, be obliged towards him" (*b*).

Quasi-contract is the act of a person, permitted by law, which obliges him towards another or obliges another towards him, without that any convention exists between them (*c*).

For example, the acceptance of a succession by an heir is a quasi-contract binding him towards the legatees. Payment of a thing through error of fact gives rise to the quasi-contract of restitution. In a contract consent is necessary to create an obligation, but in quasi-contract the law, in virtue of equity,

---

(*a*) Art. 1041.
(*b*) Art. 1042.
(*c*) Poth. Ob. 113.

establishes the obligation. In the latter it is not necessary that the person be sane or of age (*a*).

Fools cannot be bound by contract, offence or quasi-offence; because consent is necessary in all of these. But by quasi-contract they can be bound (*b*).

Arts. 1371 and 1370 of the Code Napoleon contradict each other as to a quasi-contract having a double effect. But we see by our Code that a manager and master are both, at the same time, bound and obliged by the quasi-contract *negotiorum gestio*. Our Code only gives two species of quasi-contracts, but, says Mourlon, the acceptance of a tutorship is one, also the acceptance of a succession (*c*).

Section I.—*Negotiorum-gestio*.

"He who of his own accord assumes the management of any business of another, without the knowledge of the latter, is obliged to continue the management which he has begun, until the business is completed, or the person for whom he acts is in a condition to provide for it himself . . . . He subjects himself to all the obligations which result from an express mandate" (*d*).

(*a*) Poth. Ob. 114 and 115.
(*b*) Poth. Ob. 128.
(*c*) Mour. vol. ii. No. 1661.
(*d*) Arts. 1043 to 1047.

He must exercise the care of a good administrator, and "he whose business is well managed is bound to fulfil the obligations that the person acting for him has contracted in his name."

Any one administering the business of a child: that child is obliged to give credit to that person for all his trouble and useful labour, and *vice versa* (a).

Pufendorf thinks that an oath procured by fraud is no more binding in the eyes of God than one extorted by violence. Grotius thinks an oath extorted by violence is binding, for the *will* had full sway; not so in case of fraud, because it was taken on a false supposition (b).

Gestion-d'affaires (*negotiorum gestio*) is the voluntary act of a person who, without mandate, acts, stipulates, or promises in the interest of a third party (c).

The relations between the mandator and mandatary are the same as between the administrator and the owner, except two cases. 1st. The mandatary, who does what his mandator tells him, has a right to his expenses, even if the work was of no benefit to the mandator. Not so for the administrator (*gérant*). 2nd. If the mandator dies, the mandatary is not obliged to continue the business, save in case of extreme necessity; while the administrator (*gérant*) is obliged to continue for the benefit of the heirs (d).

(a) Poth. Ob. 115.
(b) Poth. Ob. 112.
(c) Mour. vol. ii. No. 1663.
(d) Mour. vol. ii. No. 1664. Code Napoléon, arts. 1999 and 1991.

If the law is harder upon the voluntary administrator of another's business than it is on the mandatary, it is in order to keep people from meddling in the business of others.

The administrator is subject to all the obligations resulting from a contract of mandate (*a*).

The master, whose business has been well administered, is subject to all the obligations of mandate (*b*).

Two conditions are necessary in order that this quasi-contract exist.—1st. That the business be administered without the consent, express or tacit, of the master. 2nd. That the administrator did not act *animo donandi* (*c*).

There are two actions given under this source of obligations. 1st. If you administered the affairs of A., thinking them to be B.'s, you have the *actio negotiorum gestio*. 2nd. If you acted, thinking the business to be your own, you have the *actio de in rem verso* (*d*).

No further explanation is necessary for members of the Bar, and only for them does the question of the actions at law have any interest.

(*a*) Art. 1709 to 1720 C. C. L. C.

(*b*) Arts. 1720 to 1734 C. C. L. C.

(*c*) Mour. vol. ii. No. 1667; Laromb. vol. v. arts. 1372, 1373, Nos. 11, etc.; C. de Santerre, vol. v. 345; Aubry et Rau, vol. iv. sec. 411, note 2.

(*d*) Aubry et Rau, vol. iv. sec. 441, p. 725; Mour. vol. ii. No. 1668, p. 880.

Section II.—*Reception of a thing not due.*

"He who receives what is not due to him, by error of law or of fact, is bound to restore it, or if it cannot be restored in kind, to give the value of it" (*a*). The rest of this article is new law. "If the person receiving be in good faith he is not obliged to restore the profits of the thing received."

I give the new law a special attention, because it is contrary to the dispositions of the old law and the text of authorities. "He who pays a debt believing himself by error to be the debtor, has a right of recovery against the creditor." If he be in bad faith he must restore interest, profits, etc. If he received in bad faith and after being put in default he continued to keep it, he becomes answerable for its loss, even by a fortuitous event; unless it would have equally perished in the hands of its owner. Let us say a table: it was burned in the house of the holder of it—but by the same fire the owner's house was destroyed: it would have been lost in either case. If he be in good faith and sell the thing, he must restore the price of it. He to whom the thing is restored must pay the possessor, even were he in bad faith, the expenses of keeping the object in a state of preservation. For example, the feed of a horse.

In three cases does the obligation arise from this quasi-contract of reception of a thing not due.

(*a*) Arts. 1047 to 1053.

1st. When a debt that seemed to exist, but which really did not exist, has been paid through error.

2nd. When a really existing debt has been paid by the debtor to a person who seemed to be the creditor but who was not.

3rd. Finally when the debt was paid to the creditor by one who seemed to be debtor but was not (*a*).

The plaintiff, when an action is taken, upon the violation of the Obligation arising from this quasi-contract, must prove.—1st. That he intended to pay off a debt. 2nd. That the debt did not exist (*b*).

As it is impossible to enter into details of as minute a nature as I would like, I will just give an example of each of the ways in which this quasi-contract may exist and then, in the words of a French author, resume the whole theory of our law.

1st. Jones owes Smith $15 for oats and other things; it is a running account and Jones kept no record of it. He sends his son to ask Smith the amount. Smith says "fifteen dollars." The son thinks he said "fifty dollars." In consequence of the mistake Jones pays Smith's agent $50. The quasi-contract arises creating the obligation on Smith to refund, when he learns the mistake, the sum of $35 to Jones.

2nd. Jones owes $50 to Smith, but he don't know Smith personally. A man calls and asks for "that fifty dollars." Jones supposing it to be Smith pays

---

(*a*) Mour. vol. ii. No. 1672.
(*b*) *Idem* No. 1677.

him the amount. Again arises the quasi-contract and its obligations.

3rd. J. B. Jones owes Smith $5. Smith has had dealings with J. H. Jones, but J. H. Jones is not in debt to Smith. By mistake of clerk the bill is sent to J. H. Jones, instead of J. B. Jones. J. H. pays it. The quasi-contract again appears.

The whole theory is simple. No one should profit by the error of the one who pays what is not due; but, as his error is a fault, no one should suffer thereby (a).

(a) *Idem* No. 1688; Aubry et Rau, vol. iv. sec. 442, notes 37, 38 : Marc. arts. 1378-1380.

CHAPTER VI.

OF OFFENCES AND QUASI-OFFENCES.

"Every person capable of discerning right from wrong is responsible for the damage caused by his fault to another, whether by positive act, imprudence, neglect or want of skill"(a).

"He is responsible not only for the damage caused by his own fault, but also for that caused by the fault of persons under his control, and by things which he has under his care" (b). For example, the father for the child; tutors for their pupils; curators for the insane; schoolmasters for pupils; masters for servants; the owner of an animal for the damage he may do. In case of death of party, resulting from offence or quasi-offence, the heirs, within a year, can bring an action for damages.

However, a teacher is not answerable for the offence of his pupil, when he could not have prevented it or did not know of it (c).

(a) Arts. 1053 to 1057.
(b) Art. 1054.
(c) *Nullum crimen patitur is qui non prohibet, quum prohibere non potest*, L. 109, ff. de R. J.: *culpâ caret qui scit, sed prohibere non potest*, L. 50, ff. d. t.

Masters are only answerable for the offence or quasi-offence of servants when they commit them in the course of the functions for which they are employed (*a*).

There is a difference between the perpetrator of an offence and one held responsible as third party. The former in case of *contrainte par corps* may be imprisoned, while the latter can only suffer in his goods (*b*).

The offence or quasi-offence may consist in an *action* or in an *omission*. If an *action*, it must be one forbidden by law,—if an *omission*, it must be of something ordered by law. There are three conditions requisite for the existence of these sources of obligations. 1st. An illicit act. 2nd. Imputable to its author. 3rd. Causing injury or damage to another (*c*).

Let us take a few examples:

The father is answerable for the fault of his *minor child residing with him*. The law don't distinguish between emancipated and non-emancipated minors. Even for *majors residing with the father* (or in case of his death the mother), he is responsible if he is proven in fault. In the case of *minors* there is a legal presumption against parents; not so in case of majors. Minors *not with* parents, are supposed to be at school, or in the army, or under tutors, or *lawfully* absent, otherwise parents are answerable for them (*d*).

(*a*) Poth. Ob. 121.
(*b*) Poth. Ob. 122.
(*c*) Mour. vol. ii. No. 1690.
(*d*) Mour. vol. ii. No. 1692.

Even a tutor (if the child lives with him) is responsible for his conduct (a).

Let us see an example of a servant's case. A. hires B. as coachman. B. driving A.'s horse runs into a window and causes damage. A. is responsible, as he was in fault in selecting such a coachman. But B. going along meets C. (whom he hates); with a crack of his whip he puts out C.'s eye. A. is not answerable in that case. B. was not performing his duties of coachman, but going unnecessarily beyond them.

Damage caused by objects under our care. *Example:* A. owns a bull; the bull gets out and does damage; A. is answerable for it. Or again, A. owns a ship; for want of proper repairs it sinks and causes great loss to others; he is responsible to a certain degree. A *civil* and a *criminal* offence differ. In the former there must be intention—(where there is no intention it is a quasi-offence)—in the latter intention is not always necessary. *Example:* Homicide, through *imprudence*, is a *criminal* offence, for it entails a correctional penalty. It is not a *civil* offence, since there was no intention to injure (b).

I cannot agree with this opinion of Mourlon. It may be very well in French criminal law (of which I know very little), but it evidently has been the expression of a man who was ignorant of the principles of English criminal law. And, as in Lower Canada, English criminal law is that of the Province,

(a) Mour. vol. ii. No. 1693.
(b) *Idem* No. 1699: French Penal Code No. 319.

I thought well to here remark that *the intention is a sine qua non* of any criminal offence, howsoever great or small. By intention is meant the exercise of the will. When the *will* is fettered, the broad principles of British law state that there is no crime. For that reason an idiot, or an insane person, cannot commit a crime, although they may be able to perform an act that, if performed by a sane person, would be a crime. However contrary to our jurisprudence the French author's opinion may be, I introduce it here, with another object, with a view to the following distinction.

When *civil* and *criminal* actions pend in the same case, the civil must await the decision in the public or criminal tribunal. A civil action arising from a *civil and criminal* offence is prescribed by the lapse of time that prescribes a public offence; that is to say: ten, three, or one years, according as the action springs from a crime, an offence, or a mere contravention. Civil action springing from a civil offence is prescribed by thirty years (*a*).

I must once more point out the difference in French criminal law (as stated by my authority), and English criminal law. In our law there is no prescription for a crime. By Mourlon's text you would be led to believe that an action based on manslaughter (for example) would be prescribed by ten years. If it is so in French (which I doubt), it is not in English

(*a*) Mour. vol. ii. No. 1700.

criminal law. The ten years prescription would be granted *because the action sprang from a crime.* For that very reason it is not ever prescribed in our law. If a man commit murder to-day, in fifty, or even a hundred years (were he to live that long), he might be tried for the crime. I refer thus to our criminal law, in order that the reader may not be mistaken by the text of my authority and led into error.

CHAPTER VII.

OBLIGATIONS WHICH RESULT FROM THE OPERATION OF THE LAW SOLELY.

"Obligations result in certain cases from the sole and direct operation of law, without the intervention of any act, and independently of the will of the person obliged or of him in whose favor the obligation is imposed. Such are the obligations of tutors and other administrators who cannot refuse the charge cast upon them. The obligation of children to furnish the necessaries of life to their indigent parents; certain obligations of owners of adjoining properties; the obligations which in certain cases arise from fortuitous events; and others of a like nature " (a).

Such is the article of our Code and I fail to see where commentators or authorities add anything to it or serve to explain it or render it clearer than it actually is. The fact is that all obligations arise from the law. Those arising from an act of man other than a contract are either legal or illegal. If legal they give rise to a quasi-contract—if illegal to an offence or quasi-offence. I don't see the necessity of

(a) Art. 1057.

this fifth distinction. But since it exists in the Code we must take it. French authorities say that when a tutor accepts a tutorship his obligations arise from the sole operation of the law. But we have seen already that his obligations are personal and arise from quasi-contracts.

The object of this essay is not to give the opinions of every one who wrote upon obligations, it is to convey, in English, a clear idea of what obligations are, and give it as briefly as possible.

CHAPTER VIII.

OF THE OBJECT OF OBLIGATIONS.

"Every obligation must have an object." "It must be something that is an object of commerce." "It must be something determinate, at least in kind." "Future things may be the objects of an obligation."

"But a person cannot renounce a succession not yet devolved, nor make any stipulation with regard to it" (a).

"The object of an obligation must be something possible and not forbidden by law or good morals" (b).

The stipulation *triticum dare oportere*, by which the party stipulating has the option to give any quantity he desires, produces no obligation, because it can be reduced to a minimum or next to nothing. *Example:* A grain of wheat (c).

Future objects may be the object of an obligation, but are conditional. If I promise to give you next year's wheat crop and all my wheat crop is destroyed by frost or fire, the obligation vanishes (d).

(a) Arts. 1058 to 1063.
(b) Art. 1062.
(c) Poth. Ob. 131.
(d) Poth. Ob. 132.

It is evident that what is not in commerce cannot be the object of an obligation. *Example:* Church property; a public square; a bishopric, etc (*a*).

No one is bound to the impossible, therefore the object of an obligation must be something possible (*b*).

A fact contrary to law or morals is the same as an impossible one. The law *de eo quod certo loco* decides that if I promise to build you a house and no place is mentioned, there is no obligation (*c*).

Future successions cannot be the object of an obligation or contract. 1st. Because he who bargains upon a future (therefore doubtful) succession cannot know the extent of his future right or power. 2nd. Because such conventions are dangerous, as they give to third parties an interest in the death of a person stranger to them. 3rd. Because it is immoral and contains on the part of the contracting parties a *votum mortis* (or desire for the death of a party) (*d*).

The object should be—1st. Possible. 2nd. Useful to the creditor. 3rd. Not contrary to law or morals (*e*).

(*a*) Poth. Ob. 135.
(*b*) *Impossibilium nulla obligatio est.* Poth. Ob. 136.
(*c*) L. 2, sec. 5, ff. *de eo quod certo loco.* Poth. Ob. 137.
(*d*) Mour. vol. ii. No. 1095.
(*e*) *Idem* No. 1096.

CHAPTER IX.

OF THE EFFECT OF OBLIGATIONS.

SECTION I—*General Provisions*.

"An obligation to give involves the obligation to deliver the thing and to keep it safe until delivery" (*a*).

New Law.—" The obligation to keep the thing safely obliges the person charged therewith to keep it with all the care of a prudent administrator" (*b*). A creditor may also demand that what is done, in breach of obligation, be undone, if it be possible.

As this article is directly contradicted by article 1536 of the Civil Code, I will give both, in full, and point out which prevails. "Every obligation renders the debtor liable in damages in case of a breach of it on his part. The creditor may, in cases which admit of it, demand also a specific performance of the obligation, and that he be authorized to execute it at the debtor's expense, or that the contract from which the obligation arises be set aside; subject to the special provisions contained in this Code; and without prejudice, in either case, to his claim of damages" (*c*).

Article 1536 reads, "The seller of an immoveable cannot demand the dissolution of the sale by reason of

(*a*) Arts. 1063 to 1067.
(*b*) Art. 1064.
(*c*) Art. 1065.

the failure of the buyer to pay the price, unless there is special stipulation to that effect." In the Code this is marked as new law. In the case of *Richard* v. *La Fabrique de Quebec*, it was decided that article 1065 should prevail and 1536 be wiped out. I cannot agree with such a decision, when I see that 1536 is *new* law, and that in 1065 it is said, "Subject to the special provisions contained in this Code." Now, 1536 is one of those special provisions to which 1065 subjects itself. Again, 1536, being newer law, must have been created with the object of counteracting, in case of sale, the general rule laid down by 1065.

When you fail to perform something to which you are obliged your creditor cannot have you condemned *to do it*, but to *pay* damages for *not having done it* (a).

The care in conserving the object should be gauged by the nature of the contract. If the contract is *exclusively* in the interest of the creditor, the debtor is only answerable for loss of the object through *grave fault*; but if the contract is *exclusively* in his own favour, he is answerable for its loss by *slightest fault*; while, if the contract is reciprocal, he is only held responsible for loss through his *slight fault* (b).

All obligations *to do* or *not to do* resolve themselves into damages for non-fulfilment (c).

(a) Poth. Ob. 157. *Nemo potest præcisè cogi ad factum.*
(b) Mour. vol. ii. 1118; Demangeat, vol. ii. p. 522.
(c) Mour. vol. ii. No. 1138, par. 4; art. 1142, C. N.; Bug. sur Poth. vol. ii. p. 75; Marc. art. 1144; Demol. vol. i. No. 488; Aubry et Rau, vol. iv. sec. 299, p. 40, etc.

Section II.—*Defaults.*

Debtor may be put in default by lapse of term, if in the contract; by law suit; by written demand; or by sole operation of law. He is in default when the thing which he agreed to give or do could not be given or done within a certain time which he allowed to expire (*a*). The next article is new law.

"In all contracts of a commercial nature in which the time of performance is fixed, the debtor is put in default by the mere lapse of such time" (*b*).

Often the debtor is bound in damages to his creditor for failure of doing what he should have done (*c*).

In order to claim damages the creditor should prove, 1st, his claim; 2nd, the default of the debtor, and 3rd, the existence of prejudice to his interests and the amount (*quantum*) thereof (*d*).

In ancient law the debtor was not supposed to be in default except when the execution of his obligation was judicially demanded (*e*).

The obligation to give a thing, often extends to the fruits of that object (*f*).

Default is the translation of the French word *demeure*. It means to be warned of the existence of the obligation and cautioned to fulfil it or else ——.

(*a*) Arts. 1067 to 1070.
(*b*) Art. 1069.
(*c*) Poth. Ob. 147.
(*d*) Mour. vol. ii. No. 1143.
(*e*) Poth. Ob. 144.
(*f*) Poth. Ob. 145.

Section III.—*Damages.*

Damages are not due for inexecution of an obligation until the debtor is in default, except in the case of the obligation *not to do*. He is not liable to pay damages when the inexecution was due to a fortuitous event or irresistible force and not his fault. Damages due the creditor are, generally, the amount of his loss and the profit of which he was deprived. When there is no fraud, the debtor is only liable for damages which had been or might have been foreseen at time of contract (*a*). *The next is new law.*

"When it is stipulated that a certain sum shall be paid for damages for the inexecution of an obligation, such sum and no other, either greater or less, is allowed to the creditor for such damages. But if the obligation have been performed in part, to the benefit of the creditor and the time for its complete performance be not material, the stipulated sum may be reduced; unless there be a special agreement to the contrary" (*b*).

Damages from delay in payment of money, consist only of interest at the rate legally agreed upon, or fixed by law. These are due without the creditor being obliged to prove any loss. They are only due from day of default. This does not apply to bills of exchange and suretyship.

(*a*) Arts. 1070 to 1079.
(*b*) Art. 1076.

"Interest accrued from capital sums also bears interest. 1st. When there is a special agreement to that effect. 2nd. When in an action brought such new interest is specially demanded. 3rd. When a tutor has received or ought to have received interest on the moneys of his pupil and has failed to invest it within the time prescribed by law" (a).

I produce this article in full, because it is a general idea amongst people to-day that compound interest is not allowed by our law. That idea is correct as to the rule, but there are three exceptions to that rule.

Let us see a few simple examples that may illustrate the foregoing principles.

A. sells a horse to B., to be delivered on Monday. Monday comes and A. don't deliver the horse. The price of horses goes up $20. A. is obliged to pay B. the $20 difference that B. was obliged to give for another horse.

Suppose B. wanted the horse on Monday to go to town and buy a house for sale that day. In consequence of A. not delivering the horse on Monday, B. loses his chance of the house. A. is not held responsible for that. There must have been other ways of getting to town.

A. sells B. timber for a house. A. is neither carpenter, nor lumber dealer. The timber is rotten and the house falls. A. is not answerable in damages for that misfortune. B. may get the price he paid

(a) Art. 1078.

for the timber reduced. It would be otherwise if A. were a dealer in wood and knew the difference of good and bad timber.

A. sells B. a horse that has pink-eye. He don't inform B. of the fact, and in consequence B.'s horse takes the disease and dies. A. is obliged to pay B. the value thereof. But suppose that in consequence of B.'s horse dying, that B. was unable to do his spring ploughing, and had no crop that year on that account, would A. be liable for all those damages? No. Only for those damages which are the immediate consequence of the act, is he liable (a).

Even delay in execution of obligation gives rise to damages. The debtor is liable for damages,—1st. When he failed wholly, or in part, to fulfil his obligation. 2nd. When he delayed the execution of it (b).

Example.—A. sold B. a farm that belonged to E. and E. put B. off it. B. spent $100 in necessary repairs. A. is obliged to refund it to him. Now suppose B. spent $100 in ornamenting and unnecessary expenses on the farm; if A. were in good faith he is not answerable for them, but if in bad faith he must refund them to B.

If a penalty is mentioned in the agreement, the creditor will get the amount of it, and no more.

(a) All these examples are from Pothier on Obligations, Nos. 142, 143, 149, 159, 160, 161, 165, 166, 167, 170, 171, 345, 660, 668.

(b) Monr. vol. ii. No. 1154.

Pothier and Dumoulin think otherwise, but the Code Napoleon and our Code are positive.

In Roman law, compound interest was allowed, but Justinian did away with it, and the old French law and the Code also forbid it.

When there is a penalty, and the obligation was partly fulfilled, the penalty may be reduced. But not so if the creditor obtained no benefit from the partial fulfilment of the obligation (*a*).

(*a*) C. N. art. 1154; Mour. vol. ii. No. 1157; Marc. art. 1154; Dumol. vol. i. Nos. 655 et 656; *contra*, Aubry et Rau, vol. iv. sec. 308, note 58.

CHAPTER X.

DIFFERENT KINDS OF OBLIGATIONS.

SECTION I.—*Of Conditional Obligations.*

"An obligation is conditional when it is made to depend upon an event future and uncertain, either by suspending it until the event happens, or by dissolving it accordingly as the event does or does not happen" (*a*). If inconsistent with law or good morals, or if in itself impossible, or if dependent on the will of the party promising, the condition is void. No time marked for its fulfilment, it may be fulfilled at any time. The condition is broken by the party bound under it preventing it. Its fulfilment has a retroactive effect. A resolutive condition obliges each party to restore what he received, and places things as they were.

(As we proceed the details become more numerous, in proportion as the sections become more important. Upon this section of *conditional obligations*, I will give several pages from the ancient, medieval and modern writers. Its importance, I think, justifies me in so doing, for nine out of ten of our obligations are conditional.)

(*a*) Arts. 1079 to 1089.

Pothier gives us three kinds of conditions—1st. Positive. 2nd. Casual. 3rd. Mixed. An example of each—1st. I promise to give you something, if you cut down a tree in your field. 2nd. If such a ship arrives safely in England. 3rd. If you marry my cousin(*a*).

In order that a condition may suspend an obligation, it is necessary—1st. that it be the condition of something future. An obligation contracted on a past or present condition is not, properly speaking, conditional, even though the parties are ignorant of the event. So says the law, 100 ff. de vert. Oblig. (also our Code, art. 1079) (*b*).

2nd. That it be the condition of something of worth that suspends the obligation, something possible, lawful, and not contrary to good morals. If such conditions are imposed the obligation is null. *For example*, to make the obligation depend upon the fact *if you will make me a triangle without any angles;* or that you go naked in the street, etc. These are unlawful conditions (*c*).

If I agree to give you something, in case it pleases me to do so, the convention is null and void. The Romans thought that it was otherwise in case of a convention wherein I agree to give something *when I feel inclined to do so*. (L. 46, secs. 2 and 3, ff. de Verb.

(*a*) Poth. Ob. 201.
(*b*) Poth. Ob. 202; *conditio in præteritum non tantum in præsens tempus relata, statim aut perimit obligationem, aut omninó non differt;* Add. LL. 37, 38, 39, *ff. de r. cred.*
(*c*) Poth. Ob. 204.

VALIDITY OF CONDITIONS.

Oblig.) But this hair-splitting distinction cannot be admitted in our law (*a*).

There is another distinction, in the case of promise, *if I think it reasonable.* Here it does not depend on my will alone whether I am to fulfil the condition or not. If it becomes *reasonable* I must fulfil it (*b*).

That a condition be valid, it must not destroy the nature of an obligation. For example, if I promise something on condition that it pleases me—SI VALUERO —an obligation is a LEGAL TIE (*vinculum juris quo necessitate adstringimur*), and enfolds a necessity to give or to do. If the condition depends upon the will it is no longer of the essence of the obligation, but contrary to its nature. However, the condition may depend upon the will of a third party (*c*).

The condition may be something within the power of the debtor and of great interest to the creditor.

Example.—A. offers to pay B. a sum if he (B.) will cut down certain trees upon his property. B. could be summoned to elect between the two, the sum or the trees; i. e., to take or refuse the sum by cutting or refusing to cut the trees. The Romans were divided upon this. Pothier followed the Sabinian school (*d*).

A rule applicable to all conditions of obligations, is

(*a*) Poth. Ob. 47.
(*b*) *Idem* 48.
(*c*) *Idem* 205.
(*d*) *Idem* 211.

that the condition is considered to be fulfilled when the debtor has prevented its proper fulfilment (*a*).

If the creditor dies before the fulfilment of the condition, although as yet he had no real right or claim, but merely an expectation of one, and if the condition becomes fulfilled after his death, it is considered to have been transmitted to his heirs, claim, condition and all. The reason of this is that the condition of an obligation is retroactive in its effects (*b*).

An example of the above. A. has a mortgage or claim on B.'s property. The condition suspends the obligation of settling the claim. A. dies and leaves E. his heir. After A.'s death the condition is fulfilled; then E. has the same rights or claim on B.'s property that A. would have had in case he had lived.

The effect of a condition is to suspend an obligation until the fulfilment of the condition : until then there is only an expectation, not a real claim (*c*).

Therefore, payment made, in error, before the fulfilment of the condition, may be revoked. If the object of a conditional obligation perishes before the time for its fulfilment, the obligation also dies out with it (*d*).

You give or lend Peter $100 on my order. I bind myself to refund the money, *on condition* that such a

---

(*a*) *Idem* 212; *quicunque sub conditione obligatus curaverit ne conditio existeret, nihilominus obligatur;* 1, 85, sec. 7, *ff. de verb. oblig.*

(*b*) *Idem* 220.

(*c*) Poth. Ob. 218.

(*d*) *Idem* 219.

ship arrives safely in England. That is a suspensive condition, and I only become debtor when the ship has arrived. But suppose that I oblige myself towards you *until the ship* arrives in England. That is a resolutive condition. The moment the ship arrives I am no longer debtor, no matter whether she be in good order or not (*a*).

Let us turn now to more modern commentators upon these laws. Let the reader remark the harmony existing between the more ancient, the modern and our own systems.

All reál and personal rights may become conditional. It was by inadvertence that the Code, in its rubric, speaks exclusively of conditional obligations. Pothier, who treated of conditions with regard to obligations, had no need to occupy his time with conditions on *real* rights, for in his day contracts were simply productive of obligations. (Remark that this author is here speaking of the Code Napoleon, not our Code). The Code, acting like Pothier, paid no attention to the terms of articles 711 and 1138, that contracts can at one and the same time create obligations and transfer real rights. (M. Vallette) (*b*).

* * * "When an obligation depends upon an event which has actually happened, but is unknown to the parties, it is not conditional" (*c*). So says our Civil Code. Now to show how exact our Code is and

(*a*) *Idem*, 224.
(*b*) Mour. vol. ii. No. 1188 : M. Vallette.
(*c*) Art. 1079.

6

how careful the codifiers were in selecting the best authorities and most reasonable solutions of such-like questions, read the following:

The Code (Napoleon) defines a conditional obligation twice. Firstly, in art. 1168, and secondly, in art. 1181. The former says: "A conditional obligation is one that depends upon an event *future* and *uncertain*;" the latter says: "A conditional obligation is one that depends either upon a *future* and *uncertain* event or else an event which has *actually taken place, but as yet unknown to the parties*." Which of these two are we to take? The first by all means, for it agrees with the Roman law, with our old French law and with the nature of things themselves. What is a conditional obligation? It is one that *perhaps does* and *perhaps does not* exist. Therefore it is only conditional in as much as the event to which it is subject is *uncertain*. We adopt the first rule (*a*).

Therefore the part of article 1079, which I cite above, is taken from new French, old French, modern Roman and old Roman law. Pretty long pedigree; long enough to command respect!

"An obligation conditional on the will purely of the party promising is void; but if the condition consist in the doing or not doing of a certain act, although such act be dependent on his will, the obligation is

---

(*a*) Mour. vol. ii. No. 1189; Dur. vol. xi. No. 11; Bug. sur Poth. vol. ii. p. 104; Aubry et Rau, vol. iv. sec. 302 p. 62; Marc. art. 1181; Demol. vol. ii. Nos. 295 et 296.

valid" (a). This is our law: now read the French comments upon the Code Napoleon.

According to the wording of article 1174 (C. N.), the obligation contracted under an optional (potestative) condition on the part of the debtor is null. That disposition is too absolute in its terms. The obligation that depends solely (*uniquement*) on the will of the debtor is null; in this case truly no bond or *legal tie* exists. But it is not so when the obligation is subject to an event which the debtor can cause to exist or prevent from existing (b).

In the case that a condition includes a term or prefixed time in which it should be fulfilled; if it be *positive*, it is fulfilled the moment it has failed to become realized at the time prefixed; if it be *negative*, it is accomplished the moment the time is up and that the event has arrived (c).

A fulfilled condition having a retroactive effect, it results therefrom—1st. That if one of the parties to the contract dies *pendente conditione*, all its legal effects may be invoked *for* or *against* his heirs. 2nd. That the rights, servitudes, privileges, or hypothecs created *pendente conditione* by the conditional alienation of the object, are considered to be created upon the object of a third party and are therefore *null*. 3rd. That, on the other hand, all the rights created, at the same time, by the conditional acquirer, are considered

(a) Art. 1081.
(b) Mour. vol. ii. No. 1196.
(c) *Idem*, No. 1201.

to have been created by the real owner and are therefore good and valid (*a*).

A condition may fail—1st. By total loss by chance. 2nd. Partial loss by chance. 3rd. Total loss through fault. 4th. Partial loss through fault (*b*).

Resolutive condition has for effect to replace things in the same condition as they were in before. If the object of the contract is injured, *pendente conditione*, the one who is about to acquire it must suffer the loss, provided there is no fault on the part of the other. All *synallagmatical* (or double acting) contracts, (such as sale, that produces two-fold obligations), include a tacit resolutive condition. It, however, does not exist *de plein droit*, it must be proved, while ordinary resolutive conditions do take place by mere force of law, *de plein droit* (*c*).

Section II.—*Obligations with a term.*

"A term differs from a suspensive condition inasmuch as it does not suspend the obligation, but only delays the execution of it" (*d*).

It cannot be exacted before the term, but if paid voluntarily before it, without error or fraud, it cannot

(*a*) *Idem*, No. 1203.
(*b*) *Idem*, No. 1207.
(*c*) *Idem*, Nos. 1211, 1212; M. M. Val; Marcadé, art. 1183; Contrà Dur. vol. x. No. 91.
(*d*) Arts. 1089 to 1093.

be recovered. Term is presumed to be in favour of the debtor. He cannot claim it if he be bankrupt or insolvent.

A term granted by a creditor to a debtor is a proof of the former's confidence in the latter's solvency. Consequently, if that foundation fails the term ceases to exist (*a*).

When a contract is made *purely* and *simply*, nothing *suspends* the *existence*, or the *execution* of the obligation. It arises the moment the contract is passed, and is *demandable* the moment it arises. When the contract is made under *suspensive condition*, the *existence* and *execution* are both suspended. When the contract is made with a *term*, the *existence* of the obligation is not suspended, its *execution* alone is retarded, or delayed (*b*).

To pay before the term, is to pay more than you owe; to pay more than you owe, is partly to pay what you owe, and partly to pay what you do not owe (*c*).

Legal term and *grace* term differ; all that destroys the former also destroys the latter, but not *vice versa* (*d*).

Difference between *failure* (*faillite*) and *bankruptcy* (*déconfiture*). In the former case the man has merely ceased to pay his debts. *Example:* A. has $5,000 of debts; he has $8,000 in bonds which he cannot get

---

(*a*) Poth. Ob. 234.
(*b*) Mour. vol. ii. No. 1220.
(*c*) Mour. vol. ii. No. 1222; Marc. art. 1186; Demol. vol. ii. Nos. 633 et 634.
(*d*) *Idem.*

at; he *fails* to be able to meet his $5,000 of debts; demands time until he can get at his $8,000. In the second case, the man's liabilities are greater than his assets. *Example:* A. has $8,000 in money and cash, but he owes $12,000. He is bankrupt (*a*).

Section III.—*Alternative Obligations.*

"The debtor in an alternative obligation is discharged by giving or doing one of the two things which form the object of the obligation; but he cannot compel the creditor to accept a part of one and a part of the other" (*b*). *For example:* A. is bound to give B. 100 bushels of oats or 100 bushels of wheat at the end of the harvest. It may depend upon his crop which of the two he can give, and he is discharged by giving either; but he cannot oblige B. to accept 50 bushels of oats and 50 bushels of wheat.

"The option belongs to the debtor unless it has been expressly granted to the creditor" (*c*).

If one of the two things be illegal, etc., the obligation becomes pure and simple—also if one of the two things perishes. If both perished the debtor is only bound for the value of the one that remained last. Thus, suppose that oats was 30c. per bushel, and that

(*a*) Mour. vol. ii. No. 1223: see arts. C. N. 1865, 1913 and 2003.
(*b*) Arts. 1093 to 1100.
(*c*) Art. 1094.

wheat was 80c. per bushel, and the wheat first perished, the oats being the one that remained last he is only answerable for the 30c. per bushel and *vice versa*.

An alternative obligation is one whereby a party binds himself to give or to do one of two or many things, on condition that the execution of one frees him from the others (*a*).

The two or more things must be promised *disjunctively*, for if *conjunctively* there are as many different obligations as there are objects. Thus, 50 bushels of oats *or* 50 bushels of wheat, is a disjunctive or alternative obligation ; while 50 bushels of oats *and* 50 bushels of wheat is a conjunctive and forms two obligations (*b*).

If the debtor dies and leaves several heirs, each is held for his share in the object that is paid (*c*).

En resumé. 1st. If one of the two objects has perished, the debtor is responsible for the other one.

2nd. If the two have perished, one after the other, he is liable for the value of the last one.

3rd. If the two have perished through his fault, and at the same time, he is liable for the one that was the least in value.

4th. If the two have perished, at the same time, but

(*a*) Poth. Ob. 245. *Si ita stipulatus fuero decem aut quinque dari spondes, quinque debentur, l.* 12 *ff. de verb. Oblig.*

(*b*) Poth. Ob. 246.

(*c*) Mour. vol. ii. No. 1226.

without any fault on his part, he is completely free from the alternative obligation (a).

M. Bigot Préameneu says that two things being promised, there is an uncertainty as to which will be transferred, therefore no ownership is transferred by the promise, but the objects remain as the property of the debtor and at his risk until the close of the transaction (b).

Section IV—*Joint and several Obligations.*

Sub-Section I—*Joint and several Creditors.*

"A joint and several interest among creditors gives to each of them singly the right of exacting the performance of the whole obligation and thereupon of discharging the debtor" (c).

The debtor, if no suit be taken, has the option of paying to any one of the joint and several creditors. The following is new law. "Nevertheless, if one of the creditors release the debt, the debtor is discharged for the part only of such creditor. The same rule

---

(a) Mour. vol. ii. No. 1231, *bis.*

(b) M. Larombiere, vol. ii, arts. 1193, 1194, No. 2. Mourlon says that he cannot accept this system. His comments and reasons are too long to insert here. Those who wish to read them may turn to page 650 of his second volume, art. 1234, commenting upon C. N. art. 1196. I may add that I think Mourlon is wrong and the above is correct as far as our law goes.

(c) Arts. 1100 to 1103.

applies to all cases in which the debt is extinguished, otherwise than by actual payment; subject to the rules applicable to commercial partnerships" (*a*).

The effect of this joint and several quality of the creditors is fourfold. 1st. That each one being creditor for the whole, may demand the total of the obligation. 2nd. An acknowledgment of the debt made to one of the creditors interrupts the prescription for the whole debt. 3rd. Payment made to one of the creditors extinguishes the whole debt. 4th. Any one of the creditors may free the debtor completely from his debt (*b*).

The law never presumes that the claim of the creditors is joint and several. It must be proven to be so (*c*).

In order that creditors may be joint and several there are four necessary conditions: 1st. That several persons stipulate. 2nd. That they stipulate for the same thing. 3rd. That they stipulate with the same person. 4th. That they stipulate each one for the whole amount, but so that the debtor is free by paying to any one of them (*d*).

As to acts injurious to the creditors, none of them can perform them in the name of his co-creditors (*e*).

(*a*) Art. 1101.
(*b*) Poth. Ob. 260.
(*c*) Mour. vol. ii. No. 1241.
(*d*) Idem.
(*e*) *Idem*, No. 1244; Marc. art. 1199; Aubury et Rau, vol. iv. sec. 298, note 11.

SUB-SECTION II—*Of debtors jointly and severally obliged.*

Here are eighteen articles to which I call special attention. If it can be said that any one article of the Code is more important than any other one, most decidedly these eighteen are, to a certain extent, the most important, if not of the Code, at least of the Title of Obligations (a). In the first place the law that they explain is the least understood, the most often mistaken, and the most frequently applicable, of all the civil laws. I mean by this that more difficulties arise with regard to joint and several debtors than to any other class of persons. At the risk of going beyond the narrow limits which I prescribed for this essay, I shall give the articles of the Code in full and also ample explanation of them.

" There is a joint and several obligation on the part of the co-debtors when they are all obliged to the same thing, in such manner that each of them singly may be compelled to the performance of the whole obligation, and that the performance by one discharges the others towards the creditor" (b).

" An obligation may be joint and several although one of the creditors be obliged differently from the others to the performance of the same thing; for example, if one be obliged conditionally while the

(a) Arts. 1103 to 1121.
(b) Art. 1103.

obligation of the other is pure and simple, or if one be allowed a term which is not granted to the other" (*a*).

"An obligation is not presumed to be joint and several; it must be expressly declared to be so. This rule does not prevail in cases where a joint and several obligation arises of right by virtue of some provision of law;—nor is it applicable to commercial transactions, in which the obligation is presumed to be joint and several, except in cases otherwise regulated by special laws" (*b*).

"The obligation arising from the common offence or quasi-offence of two or more persons is joint and several" (*c*).

"The creditor of a joint and several obligation may apply for payment to anyone of the co-debtors at his option without such debtor having a right to plead the benefit of division" (*d*).

"Legal proceedings taken against one of the co-debtors do not prevent the creditor from taking similar proceedings against the others" (*e*).

"If the thing due have perished or can no longer be delivered, through the fault of one or more of the joint and several debtors, or after he or they have been put in default, the other co-debtors are not discharged from the obligation to pay the price of the

(*a*) Art. 1104.
(*b*) Art. 1105.
(*c*) Art. 1106.
(*d*) Art. 1107.
(*e*) Art. 1108.

thing, but the latter are not liable for damages. The creditor can recover damages only from the co-debtors through whose fault the thing has perished or can no longer be delivered, and those in default" (a).

"The rules concerning the interruption of prescription in relation to joint and several debtors are declared in the title *of Prescription*" (b).

"A demand of interest made against one of the joint and several debtors causes interest to run against them all" (c).

"A joint and several debtor sued by the creditor may plead all the exceptions which are personal to himself as well as such as are common to all the creditors. He cannot plead such exceptions as are purely personal to one or more of the other co-debtors" (d).

"When one of the co-debtors becomes heir or legal representative of the creditor, or when the creditor becomes heir or legal representative of one of the co-debtors, the confusion extinguishes the joint and several debt only for the part and portion of such co-debtor" (e).

"The creditor who consents to the division of the debt with regard to one of the co-debtors, preserves

(a) Art. 1109.
(b) Art. 1110.
(c) Art. 1111.
(d) Art. 1112.
(e) Art. 1113.

his joint and several right against the others for the whole debt" (a).

"A creditor who receives separately the share of one of his co-debtors, so specified in the receipt and without reserve of his rights, renounces the joint and several obligation with regard only to such co-debtor. The creditor is not deemed to discharge the debtor from his joint and several obligation when he receives from him a sum equal to the share for which he is bound unless the receipt specifies that it is for his share. The rule is the same with regard to a demand made against one of the co-debtors for his share, if the latter have not acquiesced in the demand, or if a judgment of condemnation have not intervened" (b).

"The creditor who receives separately and without reserve the share of one of the co-debtors in the arrears or interest of the debt, loses his joint and several right only for the arrears and interests accrued and not for those which may in future accrue, nor for the capital, unless the separate payment has been continued during [ten] consecutive years" (c).

The word ten, in brackets, denotes that it is new law—formerly, we shall see, the number of years was different.

"The obligation contracted jointly and severally towards the creditor is divided of right among the co-

---

(a) Art. 1114.
(b) Art. 1115.
(c) Art. 1116.

debtors, who among themselves are obliged each for his own share and portion only" (*a*).

"The co-debtor of a joint and several debt who has paid it in full, can only recover from the others the share and portion of each of them, even though he be specially subrogated in the rights of the creditor. If one of the co-debtors be found insolvent, the loss occasioned by his insolvency is divided by contribution among all the others, including him who has made the payment" (*b*).

"In case the creditor have renounced his joint and several action against one of the debtors, if one or more of the remaining co-debtors become insolvent, the shares of those who are insolvent are made up by contribution by all the other co-debtors, except the one so discharged, whose part in the contribution is borne by the creditor" (*c*).

"If the matter for which the debt has been contracted jointly and severally concern only one of the co-debtors, he is liable for the whole toward his co-debtors, who, with regard to him are considered only as his sureties" (*d*).

Here then is our law, as the Code gives it upon the question of joint and several debtors. By a glance at the above written articles, it will be seen that the questions arising therefrom are fraught with import-

(*a*) Art. 1117.
(*b*) Art. 1118.
(*c*) Art. 1119.
(*d*) Art. 1120.

ance and may be daily called into play. We will begin with the old law from which these principles have been gleaned and then pass on to our modern commentators.

An obligation is joint and several on the part of those who contracted it, when it binds each one for the total, in such a manner that the payment by one frees the others. Those thus obliged are called in Roman law *correi debendi* (a).

One co-debtor may be bound by a simple obligation while the others may be bound by conditional or termal, or other species of obligations (b).

The joint and several obligation may be stipulated in all kinds of contracts. But regularly it should be expressed; otherwise each one is supposed to have contracted for himself alone (c).

When commercial partners contract any obligation for the furtherance of their business, it is supposed to be joint and several, even though not expressed (d).

When several contract a joint and several obligation it is only towards the creditor that they are so bound; between themselves the debt is divisible (e).

The fact of a creditor taking action against one of the co-debtors does not free the others (f).

(a) Poth. Ob. 261.
(b) Poth. Ob. 263; L. 9, sec. 2.
(c) Poth. Ob. 265; Papinien *en loi* 11, sec. 2, *ff. de duob. reis;* Just. *la Novelle* 99.
(d) Poth. Ob. 266; Ordon. du commerce de 1673 t. 4, art. 7.
(e) Poth. Ob. 264.
(f) *Idem,* 271; L. 28 cod. *de fidej.*

For the same reason, when the object perished by the act or fault of one of the co-debtors, or since he was put in default, the debt is continued, not only against him but against the other co-debtors (*a*).

The demand made upon one co-debtor interrupts prescription against all the others (*b*).

When one of the co-debtors becomes the heir of the creditor, the debt is not extinguished against the other debtors, for according to an old principle that the confusion has effect more to clear the person of the debtor from the obligation than to extinguish the obligation itself. *Magis personam debitoris eximit ab obligatione, quàm extinguit obligationem* (*c*).

When there are more than two co-debtors, does the receipt or release given to one of them and mentioning that it is for his share destroy the joint and several nature of the obligation with regard to the other co-debtors?

I'll give an example, as the wording may not be over clear. A. B. and C. are jointly and severally obliged toward E. in the sum of $3,000. A. pays $1,000 and gets a receipt from E. stating that the $1,000 is for A.'s share; does that destroy the joint and several nature of B. and C.'s debt for the other $2,000, or are they still jointly and severally bound?

The doctors were divided upon this question. The

(*a*) Poth. Ob. 273; *ex duobus reis ejusdem Stichi promittendi, alterius factum alteri quoque nocet.*

(*b*) Poth. Ob. 272.

(*c*) Poth. Ob. 276.

ancients held to the affirmative, basing their opinion on the law *si creditores*. Pierre de L'Etoile, surnamed Stella, a famous professor at the University of Orleans, was the first, according to Alciat, who held to the negative. Bacquet, after stating that L'Etoile's opinion seems just, affirms that the contrary was followed *au Châtelet de Paris*. Pothier adds: I think it is an error that should be reformed (*a*).

When I come to our modern commentators I will point out that the error of which Pothier speaks, has been reformed and in our law L'Etoile's opinion is upheld. Even under Pothier we find the following, some three hundred and fifty numbers further on in his works: A creditor is presumed to have remitted the joint and several nature of the obligation, when he has admitted co-debtors to pay each for his own share (*b*).

When a creditor gives a receipt to a co-debtor for arrears of rent *for his share*, does he thereby discharge him for the future from his joint and several obligation? No; there is a maxim that *no one is easily presumed to give* (*c*).

Although a co-debtor who paid the whole amount has neglected to receive a subrogation, yet he is not,

(*a*) Poth. Ob. 278.

(*b*) Poth. Ob. 611.

(*c*) Poth. Ob. 279; *nemo facilé præsumitur donare;* Alciat et Bacquet.

therefore, deprived by law of his recourse against the other co-debtors for their shares in the debt (*a*).

He who got a subrogation has not only a recourse against the other co-debtors for their shares, which he paid, but also against their sureties (*b*).

This closes the list of comments, from the olden sources of law, upon this question. Be it remembered that these are but indications; I do not give more than a slight sketch and a rough plan for details; those interested may read the works indicated in these notes. Turn we to modern writers!

As a principle, when several persons promise the same thing to the same person, each of them is only *fractionally* liable. Such is common law; but it is allowed to depart therefrom (*c*).

En resumé: The joint and several debt unites in itself the following characteristics. 1st. *One single object* due by several persons and by each for *the whole*. 2nd. *One* payment freeing all the debtors. 3rd. Mandate received and given by each one of them, to represent his co-debtors (*d*.)

An obligation is not presumed to be joint and several; it must be expressly stipulated. It is only *by exception* that it takes place by operation of the law (*de plein droit*), and only in the following cases : 1st. When a widow contracts a second marriage, her second

(*a*) Poth. Ob. 282.
(*b*) Poth. Ob. 281.
(*c*) Mour. vol. ii. No. 1245.
(*d*) *Idem*, No. 1245.

husband is jointly and severally liable, with her, for the consequences of the tutorship imposed on him by the family council (art. C. N. 395 and 396). 2nd. Testamentary executors are jointly and severally liable for the account of the moveables confided to their care (art. 1033). 3rd. The surviving spouse and the subrogate tutor, in the case of art. 1442, are jointly and severally liable for the failure of an inventory. 4th. The several lessees of a house are jointly and severally liable for the losses by fire (art. 1734). 5th. In case of loan, for use, those who jointly borrow the same object are jointly and severally liable towards the lender (art. 1887). 6th. Persons owning some business between them and giving it out, by mandate, for administration, are jointly and severally liable towards the mandatary according to the rules of mandate (art. 2002). 7th. In matters of a commercial nature, such as bills of exchange, promissory notes, etc., the debt is always joint and several (arts. 22, 24, 140, 187, Code de Commerce). 8th. All parties condemned for the same crime or offence are jointly and severally liable for all damages, interests, restitutions, costs, etc., arising therefrom (art. 55, *Code pénale*) (*a*).

A debt joint and several *perfect*, procures five advantages to the creditor. It gives him the right—1st. To sue, for the whole, each one of the debtors. 2nd. To interrupt prescription with regard to the whole of them. 3rd. To put them all in default. 4th. To

(*a*) *Idem*, 1246.

make interest run against them all by a law suit taken against one of them. 5th. To be able to ask the value of the object, lost through the fault of one of them (*a*).

It happens often that several persons are jointly and severally liable although they be not co-debtors. It is the debt joint and several *imperfect* (*b*). (I cannot find any other translation for the French expression, although this fails to convey the meaning of *solidarité parfaite, et solidarité imparfaite*. Having no English noun to represent *solidarité*, I must make a circumlocution). Mourlon gives several pages on this. Thus, he says, " several persons may be held jointly and severally liable, without, however, being real co-debtors." A similar distinction exists already in the old Roman law, says Mr. Demangeat, *op. cit. p. 172 etc.* (*c*). But Mr. Demolombe does not admit that in modern French law there exists such a thing as *solidarité imparfaite*, or as I have to translate it, a debt joint and several *imperfect*. " Our theory," says he, " is that there are not two kinds of joint and several debts, the one *perfect* and the other *imperfect ;* but that there is only one kind, which arises from the law," and the learned jurist developes this theory with great vigour (vol. iii. Nos. 273, etc.). I find our law follows Demolombe's theory (*d*).

(*a*) *Idem*, 1248; Marc. vol. iv No. 593 ; Bug. sur Poth. vol. ii. p. 127.

(*b*) Mour. vol. ii. No. 1249.

(*c*) Demangeat *op. cit.*, p. 172 *et suiv*.

(*d*) Demol. vol. iii. No. 273 *et suiv*.

Let us see the exceptions that a joint and several debtor may oppose to the creditor taking action against him. I mean by exception all means proper to combat or defeat the plaintiff. The Code denotes three kinds : 1st. Exceptions resulting from the nature of the obligation. 2nd. Exceptions *personal* to one of the co-debtors. 3rd. Common exceptions (a).

The discharge of the debt is *absolute* when—1st. The creditor expressly declared it. 2nd. When he gave over his titles to one of the debtors, for when he renounces all means of proof he must naturally have renounced the claim. The discharge of the debt may be *absolute* or *relative;* it is *absolute* when the creditor renounces in favour of *all* the debtors, and is *relative* when he renounces in favour of only one (b).

There are two dispositions, taken from the same *Code Napoléon*, each the opposite of the other. How comes it they both exist? Because the codifiers gleaned their laws from two very different sources. The first comes from the subtile and strict doctrine of *acceptilation romaine*, while the second comes from the legislation of the Prætors on the *pacte de remise*. (There are no English expressions for those old terms). (c).

The *relative* discharge may be expressed or tacit. It is tacit—1st. When the creditor receiving a part payment gives a discharge in the following terms :—

(a) Mour. vol. ii. No. 1261.
(b) Mour. vol. ii. No. 1270.
(c) *Idem.* No. 1272 ; Val. Bug. sur Poth. vol. ii. p. 121; Demol. vol. iii. No. 460.

"I have received, from such a one, the sum of   , *for his share* in the debt." 2nd. When the creditor has sued one of the debtors for *his share*, and the debtor has acquiesced to that amount; or when on the same demand a judgment has intervened. The debtor who paid the whole debt has a recourse against the other co-debtors for their portions in the debt (*a*).

The actions whereby the debtor who has paid the full claim, has a recourse against the co-debtors for their shares, are—1st. A personal action—that of mandate. 2nd. The creditor's own action, with all its accessories, privileges, hypothecs, etc. The latter action he has in virtue of a legal subrogation in the rights of the creditor, taken from the principles of article 1251 (*b*).

Article 1213 C. N. says: "The joint and several obligation contracted towards the creditor, is divided by force of law, between all the debtors, who are liable towards each other only each for his part or portion" (*c*).

Extinction by compensation, confusion, etc. The authorities are so numerous, the opinions so various, the distinctions so fine, that our space will not permit of any further remarks upon this subject. However, see, for example, Vallette, Demangeat, Demolombe,

---

(*a*) Mour. vol. ii. No. 1274.
(*b*) *Idem*, No. 1280.
(*c*) *Idem*, art. C. N. 1213.

on one side; Durant, Marcadé, Aubry and Rau on the other.

It will be noticed I give, in each section, first our own law—then I commence with the Romans and trace the principles on down to the most modern French authorities.

SECTION V.—*Divisible and Indivisible Obligations.*

"An obligation is divisible when it has for its object a thing which in its delivery or performance is susceptible of division either materially or intellectually" (a).

The divisibility is not between the debtor and creditor, but between the heirs or legal representatives of one or the other. *For example*—A. owes B. $1,000. The obligation is indivisible as far as they go; but B. dies, and leaves two heirs, C. and E. The obligation becomes divisible, for A. must pay $500 to C. and $500 to E., or should it be A. that died, leaving heirs, G. and H., each of them owe $500 to B. The obligation becomes divisible. But in case of A. dying the obligation remains indivisible in the three following cases:

1st. When the object of the obligation is a certain specific thing of which one of them is in possession.

(a) Arts. 1121 to 1131.

2nd. When one of them alone is charged by the title with the performance of the obligation.

3rd. When it results either from the nature of the contract or of the thing which is the object of it, or from the end proposed by it, that the intention of the contracting parties was that the obligation should not be performed in parts (*a*).— [In the first case, he who possesses the thing due,—in the second case, he who is alone charged,—and in the third case, each of the co-heirs or legal representatives may be sued for the whole thing due; saving in all cases the recourse of the one sued against the others]. What is between brackets is new law, established by *our* codifiers.

"An obligation is indivisible—1st. When it has for its object something which by its nature is not susceptible of division, either materially or intellectually;" a horse for example. "2nd. When, although the object of the obligation is divisible by its nature, yet from the contract, this object becomes insusceptible, not only of performance in parts but also of division" (*b*).

Stipulation of joint and several liabilities does not give the obligation the character of indivisibility; each one of those who contracted an indivisible obligation is held for the whole, although they did not contract jointly and severally. The same for heirs and legal representatives. Damages from the non-performance

(*a*) Art. 1123.
(*b*) Art. 1121.

of an indivisible obligation constitutes a divisible obligation; except it be caused by fault of one of the co-heirs, when he is held indivisibly.

"Each co-heir or legal representative of the creditor may exact in full the execution of an indivisible obligation. He cannot alone release the whole of the debt, or receive the value instead of the thing itself * * * *" (a).

An heir sued for the fulfilment of an indivisible obligation may demand time to call in the other co-heirs, unless the debt be of such a nature that it can be performed only by one.

This distinction of obligations into divisible and indivisible being of very ancient origin we find much written upon the subject by the Romans and old French writers.

It is sufficient to make an obligation divisible that it be susceptible of division (b).

If the object be susceptible of intellectual division it suffices. Such is the result of the *law 9. sec. 1. ff. de salut*, where it says: *Qui Stichum debet, parte Stichi datâ, in reliquam partem tenetur*. According to this text the obligation to give the slave Stichus, is divisible, for it can be fulfilled in part although the slave cannot be divided (c).

Where the testator leaves a sum to build an hospital the obligation is divisible, because the object is money.

(a) Art. 1129.
(b) Molin. Trac. de div. et indiv. p. 3, N. 7; Poth Ob. 288, 289.
(c) Molin. *ibid*. p. 1, N. 5, p. 2, 200 et 201.

But if it says, in the will, to build in a certain place and to expend only a certain amount, then it is indivisible (a).

The obligation to perform a certain work (job), is indivisible—but not with that absolute indivisibility that Dumoulin calls "*indivisibilité contractu,*" merely the simple indivisibility of the obligation (b).

The principle that an heir is not answerable for the insolvency of his co-heirs admits of exceptions. Dumoulin points out one case where a father has two sons as heirs. One squanders *all* his share before hand, and when the succession falls the other is rendered insolvent thereby. He is held responsible for his brother's insolvency (c).

In all cases, however, the creditor cannot put the heirs of his debtor in default without making a demand on each of them (d).

When a testator leaves several kinds of heirs they are not all liable in the same manner. When the object has perished through the act or fault of several of the co-heirs, they are jointly and severally liable therefor (e).

But if each had by a special act of his own lost

(a) Loi 11, sec. 23 ; Dumoulin, p. 2, No. 368 ; Poth. Ob. 299.
(b) Poth. Ob. 298.
(c) Poth. Ob. 311.
(d) Poth. Ob. 317.
(e) Poth. Ob. 302.

a special part of the object, he would be held separately therefor (*a*).

The convention that the debt should not be payable in parts prevents the heirs of the debtor from paying in parts; but does not prevent it from being susceptible of payment in parts to the heirs of the creditor (*b*).

If the contract mentions two places of payment and uses a disjunctive, it is optional to pay in either; but if a conjunctive, it is part payable in one and part in another (*c*).

As a rule a debt cannot be paid to any one except the creditor, except with his consent (*d*).

There is a distinction between an object *individuum contractu et obligatione*: the former includes the latter. The former is the obligation of a thing, by its nature, indivisible; the latter is the obligation of a thing that, inasmuch as object of *that* obligation, is indivisible (*e*).

When the debt consists of several specific objects, the debt falls upon the debtor for part of each; not so when the objects are indeterminate (*f*).

If you left a library as deposit, although it be divi-

(*a*) Dumoulin, *qui peccavit ex eo relevari debet, quod peccati habet consortem;* Marcellus in law, 22, ff. deposit.

(*b*) Poth. Ob. 315.

(*c*) Poth. Ob. 241.

(*d*) Poth. Ob. 242.

(*e*) Poth. Ob. 293.

(*f*) Poth Ob. 322; *numero dividitur obligatio*, lex. 54, ff. deverb. oblig.; Dumoulin p. 2, No. 222.

sible, yet your heirs, or any one of them is liable for the whole (a).

Any of them through whose act or fault the object has perished, is liable for the whole (b).

From the principle, "it is one thing to give all (or the whole), and another thing to wholly give it." *Aliud est debere totum, aliud est debere totaliter*, it follows that an indivisible obligation ceases not to be subject to reduction (or retrenchment) (c).

When the obligation is indivisible, each heir of the creditor, being creditor for the whole object, it results that each of the heirs may demand the whole object from the debtor (d).

From the fact, that an heir to part of a claim that is indivisible, although creditor for the whole object, is not creditor for it *wholly* (*totaliter*), it follows that he cannot release the debt entirely, as he could were he joint and several creditor (e).

The same thing should happen when the debtor has become heir to half the claim (f).

All we have said about several heirs to an indivisible claim is applicable with regard to several creditors (not joint and several), towards whom such a debt were contracted (g).

(a) Poth. Ob. 304; lex. 3, sec. 3, ff. commod.; Molin. p. 3, N. 112.
(b) Poth. Ob. 305; Dumoul. Molin. etc.
(c) Poth. Ob. 326.
(d) Poth. Ob. 327.
(e) Lex. 13, sec. 12, ff. de accept.; Poth Ob. 328.
(f) Poth. Ob. 329.
(g) Poth. Ob. 330.

When the debt is indivisible, each heir of the debtor being debtor for the whole can be sued for the whole; but he is not *wholly* debtor—(*totaliter*), and can demand a delay to call in the co-heirs (*a*).

This is about enough for this section of the olden writers. We find in modern writers a few remarks that touch upon some phases of the question that are new.

When there only exists one creditor and one debtor, the question of divisibility or indivisibility is without effect. All obligations in themselves are indivisible as *ties of law, vinculi juris*. It is merely the exceptional nature of the obligation that gives rise to these distinctions.

Pothier remarks three kinds of divisibility—1st. Things physically and really separable—as money. 2nd. Things susceptible of parts—as a field or house. 3rd. Objects whose use is susceptible of parts—as a horse. The first and second are materially, while the third is intellectually divisible.

Dumoulin recognizes three kinds of indivisibility— 1st. *Contractû et natura.* 2nd. *Obligatione.* 3rd. *Solutione tantum.* The first case, the obligation is indivisible, *contractû et natura* when the thing that is its object, is in no way susceptible of material division; as a servitude of passage. The second case is where the object is indivisible with regard to the obligation itself, as the building of a house. The third case

(*a*) Lex 11, sec. 23, ff. de leg; Poth. Ob. 331; Dumoulin, p. 3, Nos. 90 to 104.

is where the object is really divisible, but through express or tacit convention, its execution has become indivisible; as, *for example*, I sell my house with right of redemption for $2,000. The sum becomes indivisible. The two former affect the obligation in the *active* and *passive* senses, while the last only affects it in the *passive* sense.

We see thereby that a *joint and several* obligation is not necessarily *indivisible* (art. C. N. 1219), and conversely that an *indivisible* obligation is not necessarily *joint and several* (a).

Section VI—*Obligations with a penal clause.*

"A penal clause is a secondary obligation, by which a person, to assure the performance of the primary obligation, binds himself to a penalty in case of its inexecution" (b).

The nullity of the former, save for interest, carries with it the nullity of the latter, but not *vice versa*.

The creditor may enforce the former instead of taking the penalty; but he cannot demand the two, unless the penalty be for the delay in the performance

(a) Mour. vol. ii. p. 670, sec 5, Nos. 1281 to 1301; Bug. sur Poth. vol. ii. p. 150; Val.; Aubry et Rau. vol. iv. sec. 301; Marc. arts. 1218 to 1286; Demol vol. iii. Nos. 217 to 236; Dur. vol. xi. Nos 276 to 290.

(b) Arts. 1131 to 1138.

of the former obligation. No penalty due until the debtor is in default. The next article is new law.

"The amount of penalty cannot be reduced by the court; but if the obligation have been performed in part to the benefit of the creditor, and the time fixed for its complete performance be not material, the penalty may be reduced; unless there is a special agreement to the contrary" (a).

"When the primary obligation contracted with a penal clause is indivisible, the penalty is incurred upon the contravention of it by any one of the heirs or other legal representatives of the debtor; and it may be demanded in full against him who has contravened it, or against each one of them for his share and portion, and hypothecarily for the whole; saving their recourse against him who has caused the penalty to be incurred" (b).

When the primary obligation is divisible, the penalty is only incurred by the one of the heirs of the debtor who contravenes the obligation; save and except when the penal clause was added with the intention that payment could not be made in parts.

It must be agreed that the heir who contravenes an indivisible obligation contracted by the deceased, becomes debtor for the whole of the penalty (c).

The penal obligation being the accessary of the other, it follows that, if the original obligation be-

---

(a) Art. 1135.
(b) Art. 1136.
(c) Poth. Ob. 357; Dumoulin, p. 3, Nos. 173 et 174.

comes null, so likewise does the penal one; except when he towards whom the obligation was contracted, has no special interest in it (*a*).

The nullity of the penal obligation does not cause the nullity of the original obligation, on the principle that the principal can exist without its accessary (*b*).

The end for which the penal clause is created, is to secure the fulfilment of the original obligation (*c*).

The penal clause does not destroy the right of action for the non-fulfilment of the obligation, nor the *exceptions et fins de non recevoir* (*d*).

The rule that the principal obligation and the penalty cannot be both asked, suffers exception in the case where the obligation should have been fulfilled in a certain term; example: A. is obliged towards B. to build his house in three months, and should he not do so, to give B. $100. If at the end of three months the house is not built, B. can demand the $100, and still demand of A. to complete the house (*e*).

The principle that the penalty is only due in proportion to the non-fulfilment of the obligation, holds good even in case of an indivisible obligation (*f*).

(*a*) Poth. Ob. 339 et 340; *Quàm causa principalis non consistit, ne ea quidem quæ sequuntur locum obtinent*; lex. 129, sec. 1, *ff. de regul. jur.*

(*b*) Poth. Ob. 341; lex 97, *ff. de verb oblig*; Paul on the law, 126, sec. 3; *Detractâ primâ stipulatione, prior memet utilis.*

(*c*) Poth. Ob. 342.

(*d*) Poth. Ob. 344.

(*e*) Poth. Ob. 345.

(*f*) Poth. Ob. 355 et 356; Paul, lex. 85, sec. 3, *ff. d. tit*; Cato, lex 4, sec. 1, *ff. d. verb oblig.*

CATO'S THEORY AND EXAMPLE. 97

When the obligation contracted under penal clause is of an indivisible thing, the contravention thereof by one of the heirs of the debtor leaves, not only him, but all the other co-heirs open to the penalty ; save their recourse against each other (a).

All said about heirs to a debtor, refers to all joint and several debtors (b).

When the original obligation, under penal clause, has for its object a divisible fact, Cato seems to decide that the one, of the heirs of the debtor, who failed in the obligation, is alone liable for the penalty as far as his share goes (c).

Cato says that the heir who breaks the obligation, while the others are ready to fulfil it, is bound towards the creditor only for *his own* share of the penalty, but is also bound towards the other co-heirs or co-debtors for their shares of the penalty (d).

I'll give an example here of Cato's theory. A., B. and C. are bound to build a house for H. If it is not completed in three months they are bound to the penalty of $300. B. and C. wish to finish the house in time, but A. prevents them. If the house is not completed at the expiration of the three months, A.

(a) Poth. Ob. 306; Molin, p. 3, Nos. 439 et 440; Paul, lex. 17, sec. 2, *commod*.

(b) Poth. Ob. 359.

(c) Poth. Ob. 360; Cato *si de eo cautum sit quod divisionem recipiat, veluti ampliùs non agi, eum hæredem qui adversùs ea facit, pro portione suâ solûm pænam committere*. Cujas and Dumoulin are of the same opinion.

(d) Poth. Ob. 361.

8

is only bound towards H. for his own share of the penalty, $100; but he is bound toward B. and C. for their respective shares in the penalty—that is $100 to each of them.

Mourlon calls the penal clause a forfeit. Is the penalty suffered, for the whole, by each of the co-heirs when only one is in fault? Pothier and the Code Napoleon distinguish two cases—1st. When the principal obligation is indivisible. 2nd When it is divisible.

1st. The penalty (these are the words of the Code Napoleon) is incurred by the contravention of one of the heirs of the debtor, and may be demanded *wholly* off him, or else off each of the other co-heirs, each for his share and portion, save their recourse against the party in fault. Mourlon says this is borrowed from Pothier, and he criticises it very severely. [I think Mourlon is a little, if not very much astray. As is seen by the foregoing that Pothier drew this principle from Cato, the greatest of Roman authorities, and has sanctioned it himself, as has likewise Dumoulin. The Code Napoleon, article 1232, reproduces it; Marcadé and Demolombe sanction its adoption in the Code Napoleon, and our Civil Code of Lower Canada reproduces it again, word for word, in article 1136. Consequently, I think Mourlon stands alone in this case, and exact as he is in general and great authority as he may be, I cannot see how his opinion could for a moment be entertained, when it appears alone against such an array of authorities, from Cato to our own Code.]

2nd. The penalty is only undergone by the heir of the debtor who contravened the obligation, and only for his share (*a*).

(*a*) C. N. 1226 to 1234; Mourlon, 1302 to 1306; Marc. art. 1226 to 1234; Demol. vol. iii. No. 700.

CHAPTER XI.

EXTINCTION OF OBLIGATIONS.

Section I.—*General Provisions.*

"An obligation becomes extinct: by payment, by novation, by release, by compensation, by confusion, by the performance of it becoming impossible, by judgment of nullity or rescission, by the effect of the resolutive condition, which has been explained in the preceding chapter, by prescription, by the expiration of the time limited by law or by the parties for its duration, by the death of the creditor or debtor in certain cases, by special causes applicable to particular contracts, which are explained under their respective heads" (*a*).

The Code Napoleon, article 1234, contains the very same as the above. Speaking of the resolutive condition, Mourlon seems to think that it should not be ranged amongst the modes of extinction of obligations; he says it is both *productive* and *extinctive* of obligations, according as it exists *after* or *before* the execution of the contract which it modifies (*b*). (I cannot

(*a*) Art. 1138.
(*b*) Mour. vol. ii. No. 1306, sec. 2.

again agree with him, for an article of his own Code, (1603), proves that in all cases, whether *before* or *after*, the resolutive condition extinguishes the obligation of *garantie*. See our Code, Art. 1491. The seller has two obligations; "1st, the delivery; and 2nd, the warranty of the thing sold." Suppose then the case given by Mourlon (page 686). A. sells B. a horse for $100, upon resolutive condition. The condition is fulfilled, and A. is thereby obliged to refund the $100, and B. to give back the horse. Mourlon argues that the resolutive condition gives birth to two new obligations but does not extinguish any old one. But does it not extinguish A.'s old obligation of warranty? Here again does Mourlon run foul of the two Codes and of legal logic. I might as well say that *prescription* could not be a mode of extinction of obligations, because it is a mode of creation of obligations. We must remember that prescription is a double-acting machine —*une épée à deux tranchants*. "It is (says our Code at Art. 2183) a means of *acquiring* or of *being discharged* by lapse of time." It is positive and extinctive both. Might I not then as well say that prescription cannot be a mode of extinction of obligations, as for Mourlon to say that the resolutive condition should not be classed amongst those means of extinction?

While I am thus in parenthesis, let me remark that *payment*, the subject of the next section, deserves a most special attention. It is the most usual and most frequently disputed mode of extinction of obligations).

Section II—*Payment.*

Sub-Section I—*General provisions.*

"By payment is meant not only the delivery of a sum of money in satisfaction of an obligation, but the performance of anything to which the parties are respectively obliged" (a).

Payment presupposes a debt, otherwise it may be recovered. It may be made by any one, even a stranger. "If the obligation be to do something which the creditor has an interest in having done by the debtor himself, the obligation cannot be performed by a stranger to it without the consent of the creditor" (b). *For example*: A. hires B. to build his house, unless A. consents, B. cannot get E. to do it. A. may have a confidence in B. that he has not in E.

The payor must have a legal right to the thing he pays. If money or something consumable, it cannot be recovered from the payee who has used it. Payment must be to the creditor or some one authorized by him, or by law to receive it. If made in good faith to an ostensible creditor, is valid. If made to one incapable of receiving by law, it is not valid, unless the debtor proves that it turned to the creditor's benefit. Payment made to the prejudice of a seizure is not valid against the seizing creditor, and the

---

(a) Arts. 1139 to 1154.
(b) Art. 1142.

debtor may be forced to pay it again—with recourse against the creditor so paid. The creditor cannot be compelled to receive anything other than the thing due to him.

"A debtor cannot compel his creditor to receive payment for his debt in parts, even if the debt be divisible. [Nor can the court in any case by its judgment order a debt actually payable to be paid by instalments without the consent of the creditor;" (a). The part in brackets is new law.

Debtor of a specific thing is discharged by the delivery of it in the condition in which it is at the time of payment, unless through his fault it became deteriorated.

"If the object of the obligation be a thing determined in kind only, the debtor cannot be required to give a thing of the best quality, nor can he offer in discharge one of the worst. The thing must be of a merchantable quality" (b).

Payment must be made at the place indicated. If no place mentioned and the object be a specific thing, it must be made where the thing was at time of contracting the obligation. In all cases it must be made at the domicile of the debtor, subject to rules in contracts.

"The expenses attending payment are at the charge of the debtor" (c).

(a) Art. 1149.
(b) Art. 1151.
(c) Art. 1153.

Such are, in full, the principles of our Code upon the general provisions of payment; now we turn to comments and explanations.

Payment is the accomplishment of what we are obliged to give or to do. If voluntarily made it cannot be recalled, but it is redeemable when made in error (*a*).

No matter who makes the payment, the obligation is extinguished (*b*).

Can a complete stranger to the obligation, one who has no interest in it, compel the creditor to accept payment? Not if the payment be the doing of something which the creditor has an interest in having done by the debtor himself (*c*).

Payment is null if the payor does not own the object, or if he has no right to give it. A sum of money spent in good faith, by the creditor, he having received it from one who had no right to it, makes the payment good (*d*).

(I don't believe this principle, nor do I think our article 1143 really reproduces it. If it does, our article requires another clause. When I come to the modern commentators and have given their opinions, I shall explain why I think this to be unjust).

(*a*) Poth. Ob. 494, 195, 218.
(*b*) Caius in legem 53, *ff. de solut;* Poth. Ob. 499.
(*c*) Poth. Ob. 500.
(*d*) Poth. Ob. 495, 497, 498; *nemo plus juris in alium transferre potest quàm ipse habet,* L. 54, *ff. de reg juris.*

Payment of a thing is only made by transfer to the creditor of the ownership thereof (a).

Payment made to one authorized by the creditor to receive it, is supposed to have been made to the creditor himself (b).

Often we suppose a person to be the real creditor when he is not; payment then made to such a one is valid (c).

Our article 1148, and Pothier, No. 530, are in contradiction to the *Novel.* 4, cap. 3, that permits a debtor to compel a creditor to receive something other than what is due him.

In the broad sense payment is the extinction of an obligation; in the narrower acceptation it is the accomplishment of an obligation. "Every payment supposes a debt," is a phrase that has a two-fold importance—1st. The payment is null if the debt it was supposed to clear did not exist. 2nd. By the fact of a payment the debt is presumed to have been a real one, unless proof to the contrary be forthcoming (d).

Every payment supposes a debt, therefore what has been paid for a debt that did not exist may be recovered—all paid that is not due may be recovered (e).

(a) *Non videntur data quae eo tempore quo dantur accipientis non fuint,* L. 167, *ff. de r. juris.*

(b) Poth. Ob. 501, 508, lex. 108 ; *quod jussu alterius solvitur, pro eo est quasi ipsi solutum esset.*

(c) Poth. Ob. 503.

(d) Mour. vol. ii. No. 1307.

(e) M. M. Bigot Préameneu and Jaubert; Demol. vol. iv. Nos. 29 to 31.

A payment made by one who need not have made it to one who had no right to demand it the law declares valid. It is not considered as a *donation* but as a *payment*. Mourlon enters into a splendid discussion upon the proving that the word *naturelles* should be *civiles*. The article reads: "The recovery of a payment made voluntarily is not allowed in cases of *natural* obligations." Massol agrees with Mourlon, that the word *natural* should be *civil*. But Demolombe contradicts this pretention (*a*), while Aubry and Rau support Mourlon's (*b*).

Were it not for want of space I would like to enter into the question more fully. I think Mourlon is right. See Mourlon, vol. ii. page 688 and following. When the codifiers were casting their plans for the Code Napolèon, it was thus they made that unfortunate article read: "The right to recovery ceases with regard to those *debts for which the one obliged might have refused payment in consequence of an exception and which he paid voluntarily.*" If this text had been preserved the difficulty would not exist.

By whom should payment be made? 1st. Payment made by the debtor—the debt is extinguished with all its accessories. 2nd. Payment made by a third party interested in the extinction of the debt—a surety for example—it is accompanied, *de plein droit*, with subrogation. The third party, paying it, has two

---

(*a*) Demol. vol. iii. No. 38 and vol. iv. Nos. 41 and 42.

(*b*) Aubry et Rau, vol. iv. sec. 297; Mour. vol. ii. Nos. 1307, 1308 and above all 1309.

actions for his recourse—1st. A personal action of mandate or *gestio negotiorum*. 2nd. The ordinary creditor's action. 3rd. Payment made in the name and to the knowledge of the debtor by a third party, stranger to the debt, that payment is not *de plein droit* accompanied with subrogation. The payor has only a simple action of *negotiorum gestio*. 4th. Payment made, *in his own name*, by a stranger to the debt, extinguishes the debt and all its accessories; but the one paying has, against the debtor, merely an action *de in rem verso* (a).

To whom should payment be made? 1st. To the creditor himself, if he is capable of receiving. 2nd. To his mandatary. 3rd. To the possessor of the claim. All other payments are null (b).

What must be paid? The thing due. The creditor cannot be forced to accept anything else, unless an agreement is to the contrary (c).

In principle the debtor cannot force the creditor to take part payments, yet the creditor must accept them from the heirs of the debtor.

Where should payment be made? 1st. When a place is agreed upon, it must be there. 2nd. If no place be agreed upon, it must be paid at the place where the object was at the time of agreement. 3rd. If neither of these two cases exist, it is to be made at the debtor's place. Expenses of payment are to the

---

(a) *Idem*, No. 1316.
(b) *Idem*, No. 1330.
(c) *Idem*, 1337 to 1349.

debtor's charge, but the expenses of carrying away the object are payable by the creditor (a).

Now I come to what I referred to a few pages back. Let me just repeat Pothier and our Code. Pothier says: "A sum of money spent, in good faith, by the creditor, he having received it from one who had no right to it, makes the payment good." The fact of spending the money *in good faith* makes the payment good. Now see what the second clause of our article 1143 says: "If a sum of money or other thing of a nature to be consumed by use be given in payment, it cannot be reclaimed from the creditor who has used it in good faith, although the payment have been made by one who was not the owner nor capable of alienating it."

Despite Pothier, the Code Napoléon (art. 1238), and the Civil Code of Lower Canada (art. 1143), I fail to see the justice of this law, nor do I believe it is the law. It is incomplete. I will illustrate it by an example, and the injustice of the dispositions will be apparent.

A. owes B. a ton of hay. Not having a ton to give to B. when the time for payment comes, he takes a ton of E.'s hay and pays his debt to B. with it. B. in good faith, believing the hay to belong to A., feeds it out to his horses and they consume it. The law as above says that it cannot be reclaimed from B. That is the case in our Code. Then is E. to lose his ton of

---

(a) *Idem*, No. 1352. See Marcalé and Colmet d'Aage and Bonnier on this.

hay, and A. to profit thereby to clear his debt, and still E. to have no recourse? Says Mourlon, on this, "Our article 1238 does not regulate the relations between the creditor who received and the person to whom the thing belonged. We must turn to the common law for the decision." And the common law regulates that E. can get it back, or the value of it from A. or B. I think these articles both of our Code and the Code Napolèon should contain another clause regulating this point.

Permit me an example upon Pothier's statement. A. is a minor, with no right to dispose of his money. B. owes E. a debt of $100 and A. pays it for him. A. had no right to spend the $100, but E. *in good faith* got rid of the money. Now, according to Pothier, the fact of E. being in good faith when he spent the money, makes the payment valid. At once you can see the fallacy of the presumption. How can an action, howsoever good or bad the faith of the actor may be, render valid what is radically null? The payment being null *ab initio*, there is no fiction of law that can make it exist. It would be to draw something from nothing; to make a dead being revive.

Sub-Section II.—*Payment with Subrogation* (a).

The Code does not define subrogation. It is the substitution of a third party in the rights of a creditor

(a) Arts. 1154 to 1158.

against a debtor whose debt that third party has paid. It is either conventional or legal. It is necessary to give the two principal articles in full.

"Subrogation is conventional: 1st. When the creditor, on receiving payment from a third person, subrogates him in all his rights against the debtor. This subrogation must be express and made at the same time as the payment. 2nd. When the debtor borrows a sum for the purpose of paying his debt, and of subrogating the lender in the rights of the creditor. It is necessary to the validity of the subrogation in this case, that the act of loan and the acquittance be notarial, [or be executed before two subscribing witnesses;] that in the act of loan it be declared that the sum has been borrowed for the purpose of paying the debt, and that in the acquittance it be declared that the payment has been made with the moneys furnished by the new creditor for that purpose. This subrogation takes place without the consent of the creditor. [If the act of loan and the acquittance be executed before witnesses, the subrogation takes effect against third persons from the date only of their registration, which is to be made in the manner and according to the rules provided by the law for the registration of hypothecs]" (a).

"Subrogation takes place by the sole operation of law and without demand—1st. In favour of a creditor who pays another creditor whose claim is preferable

(a) Art. 1155.

to his by reason of privilege or hypothec. 2nd. [In favour of a purchaser of immoveable property who pays a creditor to whom the property is hypothecated. 3rd. In favour of a party who pays a debt for which he is held with others, or for others, and has an interest in paying it]. 4th. In favour of a beneficiary heir who pays a debt of the succession with his own moneys. 5th. When a rent or debt due by one consort alone has been redeemed or paid with the moneys of the community; in this case the other consort is subrogated in the rights of the creditor according to the share of such consort in the community " (*a*).

These subrogations have effect against sureties. It cannot prejudice the remaining rights of the creditor when he has received only part payment.

Dumoulin and Pothier are at war upon the question of tacit subrogation. We have not space to enter into their quarrel, but our article 1156 settles the question as far as we have an interest direct in it.

Whosoever pays a debt for another has a right, in paying, to get the action of the creditor against the debtor. Upon this principle Julian goes when referring to the rights of the *fidéjusseur* (*b*).

Payment extinguishes a debt, but subrogation transfers it to another. Here are two very incompat-

(*a*) Art. 1156.
(*b*) Poth. Ob. 556; *Fidejussoribus succurri solet, ut stipulator compellator ei qui solidum solvere paratus est vendere cæterorum nomina*; l. 17, ff. *fidejus.*

ible ideas. The Romans perceived them, but were not stopped by the seeming contradiction; they settled the affair by their old and ordinary means when in a corner, that is by a *fiction of law*. The creditor is *presumed to have sold* his claim to the one subrogated, who is *supposed to have purchased it* (*a*).

Pothier says subrogation is a *fiction of law* by means of which a creditor is supposed to cede his rights to a third party who has paid him.

The party subrogated may invoke it against—1st. The debtor, in order to have against him all the means that comprise the paid debt, such as a penal clause, etc. 2nd. Against the debtor's creditors, to exclude them by opposing to them the privileges, etc., obtained. 3rd. Against the sureties. Our art. 1157, C. C. L. C., mentions this also, because it was not admitted by the Roman jurists. 4th. Against third parties holding the hypothecated immoveables thus bound for the payment of the debt (*b*).

According to this system we may define a subrogation as follows : A fictive cession, in consequence of which a claim extinguished by means of a payment with the money of a third party is looked upon as continuing to exist to the benefit of the latter, who

---

(*a*) Mour. vol. ii. No. 1354; C. N. 1249: *non in solutum accepit, sed quodammodo nomen debitoris vendidit* (Paul. L. 36, D. de fidej.): *non est vera cessio*, says Renusson, *sed cessio fictiva*.

(*b*) Mour. vol. ii. No. 1359

may exercise it to recover thereby what it cost him to free the debtor (a).

M. M. Merlin and Grappe, whose doctrine was reproduced by M. Bugnet and also by Marcadé, teach another system. With them subrogation is "the attachment, conventional or legal, of the accessories, privileges, hypothecs and sureties, of the old claim extinguished by payment with the money of a third party, to a new claim arising from the payment or loan that procured to the debtor the means whereby to free himself" (b).

In the first system, the subrogation transfers to the one subrogated the claim and all its accessories, privileges, etc. In the second system, it detaches the accessories of the old claim that payment has extinguished, and attaches them to the new claim arising therefrom. We must reject the latter system as contrary to—1st. The authority of history, (see ordonnance of 1609). 2nd. To the terms of the law in the Code. 3rd. To the end which the law had in view in organizing the system of subrogation (c).

All subrogations come from the law (d). Subrogation consented to by the *creditor* should be *express* and made at the time of payment. Thus two con-

---

(a) *Idem*, No. 1360; M. M. Val.; Aubry et Rau, vol. iv. sec. 321; Larombière, art. 1249; Colm. de Saint, vol. v. No. 189; Demol. vol. iv. No. 325. This system was first formulated by Mr. Ferry, at Paris.

(b) Mour. vol. ii. No. 1360.

(c) *Idem*, No. 1361.

(d) *Idem*, No. 1365.

ditions—1st. Express declaration of subrogation. 2nd. Payment and subrogation to be simultaneous (*a*).

. Subrogation consented by the debtor to the benefit of a third party who lent him the means to pay the debt. It must—1st. Have the acts establishing the loan and payment, both in notarial form. 2nd. It must be mentioned in the act of loan, that the money is borrowed to pay the claim; and in the act of payment that it is made with money so borrowed. Read the note to this particularly; it has an historical interest (*b*).

Subrogation from sole operation of the law is an exception. In four cases it can arise—1st. To the benefit of the one who was creditor and paid the debt to another creditor who had been preferred to him by privilege or by hypothec. 2nd. To the benefit of the one acquiring an immoveable, who spent his

---

(*a*) *Idem*, No. 1366.

(*b*) *Idem*, No. 1367. Subrogation by the debtor was introduced by the Edict of 1609, under Henri IV. The origin of it is amusing. Under Charles IX. the run of interest was 8¼ per cent., while Henri IV. reduced it to 6¼. The debtors under the Charles IX. system looked out for money lenders from whom they could get the money at the lower rate of 6¼, and pay off therewith their old and heavy debt of 8¼. But these capitalists demanded securities that the debtors, in most part, could not furnish. The power to transfer to the new creditor their securities (garanties) could procure for them credit to get the new loan. But this subrogation not being possible without the consent of the first creditors, and they refusing that consent, made it impossible for the debtors to take advantage of the 6¼ interest. Henri IV., anxious to help them, gave them the right of subrogation without the creditors' consent.

own money to pay off the hypothecs that were on it (*a*). 3rd. To the benefit of one who was held *with* or *for* others in a debt, and who has an interest in clearing it off. 4th. To the benefit of the beneficiary heir who pays with his own money the debts of the succession (*b*).

On the whole I think the simple definition that I give at the opening of this sub-section, covers the entire ground.

Sub-Section III.—*Imputation of Payment.*

"A debtor of several debts has a right of declaring, when he pays, what debt he means to discharge." "A debtor of a debt that bears interest or produces rent cannot without the consent of the creditor impute any payment which he makes to the discharge of the capital, in preference to the arrears of interest or of rent. Any payment made on the capital and interest, but which is not entire, is imputed first upon the interest" (*c*). When a debtor of several debts accepts a receipt imputing the discharge to be for a special debt, he cannot demand that it be imputed to the other debt. "When the receipt imputes no special debt, it is supposed to be for the debt which the debtor had most interest to pay. But if one of the debts be actually payable it must be considered paid, although

---

(*a*) Mour. vol. ii. Nos. 1370, 1371, 1372 and 1373; Caqueray Rev. Prat. vol. vi. p. 81.

(*b*) Barillet, D. L. L. Rev. Prat. p. 20, vol. xiv.

(*c*) Arts. 1158 to 1162.

it be less burdensome than the other. If they be all equally burdensome and equally payable, the payment is imputed upon the oldest debt. All things being equal it is made proportionally on each " (*a*).

He who is creditor of a person for different debts is obliged to receive the payment which his debtor offers him of one of the debts, even though he does not offer him, at the same time, payment of the other (*b*).

If the different debts be of equal date, and all other things are equal, the imputation is made proportionally on each (*c*).

In debts that produce interest, the payment is imputed to be on the interest before the capital (*d*).

When the debtor makes no imputation, the creditor may make it, in the receipt, provided it be made then and there and be equitable (*e*).

Sometimes the creditor can be forced to accept what is not due him, but only when the power is given to the debtor by agreement (*f*).

Imputation may be made—1st. By the debtor. 2nd. By the creditor. 3rd. By the law.

1st Case.—The debtor may impute as he pleases, except in three cases, viz:—1st. On a debt greater than

---

(*a*) Art. 1161.
(*b*) Poth. Ob. 539.
(*c*) Idem, 569: *si par et dierum et contractuum causa sit, ex summis omnibus solutum;* lex 8, ff. de solut.
(*d*) Poth. Ob. 570: *Primo in usuras, id quod solvitur, deinde in sortem, accepto feretur;* l. 1, Cod. hoc tit.
(*e*) Poth. Ob. 566.
(*f*) *Idem*, 530.

the sum he offers, for a creditor cannot be forced to accept partial payment. 2nd. On a debt not due when the term is stipulated by the creditor. 3rd. On the *capital* in preference to the *interest*.

2nd Case. — When the debtor confides to the creditor the imputation, he tacitly confirms the creditor's choice, unless there be fraud proved against the creditor.

3rd Case. — When neither creditor nor debtor impute, the law traces the following rules—1st. When one debt is due and the other not, payment is imputed on the debt due. 2nd. When both are equally demandable, it is imputed on the one which the debtor has most interest in paying. 3rd. When there is no difference, it is on the oldest debt, and if none is oldest, it is proportionally divided (*a*).

SUB-SECTION IV.—*Tender and Deposit.*

When a creditor refuses to receive payment, the debtor may make a tender of the money or the thing due; and if an action be brought afterwards the debtor has only to renew the tender by actual deposit of the sum or thing and it is equivalent to a payment made when the first tender was made, provided that since the date of the first tender he was always willing to pay (*b*).

"It is necessary to the validity of a tender—1st. That it be made to a creditor legally capable of receiv-

(*a*) Mour. vol. ii. Nos. 1376, 1377. 1378.
(*b*) Arts. 1162 to 1169.

ing payment or to some one having authority to receive for him. 2nd. That it be made on the part of a person legally capable of paying. 3rd. That it be of the whole sum of money or other thing payable, and of all arrears of rent and interest, and all liquidated costs, with a sum for costs not liquidated, saving the right to make up any deficiency in the same. 4th. That, if it be of money, it be made in coin declared by law to be current and a legal tender. 5th. That the term of payment have expired if stipulated in favour of the creditor. 6th. That the condition under which the debt has been contracted has been fulfilled. 7th. That the sum of money or other thing tendered be offered at the place where, according to the terms of the obligation or by law, payment should be made "(a).

"[If, by the terms of the obligation or by law, payment is to be made at the domicile of the debtor, a notification in writing by him to the creditor that he is ready to make payment has the same effect as an actual tender, provided that in any action afterwards brought the debtor make proof that he had the money or thing due ready for the payment at the time and place when and where the same was payable]" (b).

"If a certain specific thing be delivered on the spot where it is, the debtor must by his tender require the creditor to come and take it there." If it be something difficult to transport, he must name the day and place where he will be ready to deliver it. If the

(a) Art. 1163.
(b) Art. 1164.

creditor fail to take it away, or to accept it, the debtor may put it any place in safe keeping. As long as the creditor has not accepted the tender and deposit, the debtor may withdraw them by leave of court. When tender and deposit have been declared valid by the court the debtor cannot withdraw them, even with the creditor's consent, to the prejudice of his co-debtors or sureties.

The effect of tender and deposit is that, when it is declared valid by the court, the debtor is freed from his debt and is still—*subtilitate juris*—owner of the money or thing until the creditor takes it away (*a*).

Tender and deposit is not a real payment, for it is not a transfer of the property to the person of the creditor (*b*).

A debtor has a great interest in discharging his debt, for if it be a specific thing, he has the expense of its keeping—as a horse; if it be money, it is at his risk. When the creditor refuses to let him clear his debt, the law gives him the "Tender and Deposit" (*c*).

If the creditor refuses the tender, the debtor can get a *proces verbal* drawn up and served by a bailiff upon the creditor, demanding him to appear such a day and accept the tender. If he refuses still, the debtor is free from his debt, and all right of action against him dies out (*d*).

(*a*) Poth. Ob. 580.
(*b*) *Idem*, 573: *Dominium non acquiritur nisi corpore et animo.*
(*c*) Mour. vol. ii. No. 1379.
(*d*) *Idem.*

1st. Debts of sums of money. 2nd. Debts of specific things. 3rd. Debts having for object, something undermined, other than a sum of money. Let us see each of these.

1st case.—See above, article 1163 of our Code as to the conditions for the validity of the tender ; as to the deposit—1st. A summons served on the creditor, naming the day, hour and place of deposit. 2nd. That the debtor give up the sum then and there. 3rd. A *proces verbal* of the objects deposited. 4th. That in case of the non-appearance of the creditor, he be summoned to withdraw the deposit.

2nd case.—Things not transferable, etc., cannot be deposited. Then summon the creditor to come and take them in a certain place.

3rd case.—Most of the authors adopt the procedure of case No. 2. There is much on this in the Code of Procedure (*a*).

SECTION III.—*Novation.*

" Novation is effected—1st. When the debtor contracts towards his creditor a new debt which is substituted for the ancient one, and the latter is extinguished. 2nd. When a new debtor is substituted for a former one who is discharged by the creditor.

(*a*) *Idem*, 1380; Dur. vol. xii. No. 221; Marc. art. 1257; Aubry et Rau, vol. iv. sec. 322. Read Mourlon, vol. ii. Nos. 1391 to 1395.

3rd. When by the effect of a new contract, a new creditor is substituted for a former one towards whom the debtor is discharged " (a). The parties must be capable of contracting. It is not presumed. When by the substitution of a new debtor, it may be with the concurrence of the former one. Simple indication of a party to pay the debt does not constitute novation. Privileges, etc., do not become transferred from the old to the new debt unless expressly stated.

" Joint and several debtors are discharged by novation effected between the creditor and one of the co-debtors. Novation effected with respect to the principal debtor discharges the sureties. Nevertheless, if the creditor have stipulated in the first case, for the accession of the co-debtors, and in the second, for that of the sureties, the ancient debt subsists if the co-debtors or the sureties refuse to accede to the new contract " (b).

" The debtor consenting to be delegated, cannot oppose to his new creditor the exceptions which he might have set up against the party delegating him, although at the time of the delegation he were ignorant of such exceptions " (c).

This don't apply where at time of delegation nothing was due to the creditor.

(a) Arts. 1169 to 1181.
(b) Art. 1179.
(c) Art. 1180.

The Code gives no real definition of novation; it is the substitution of a new debt for an old one (*a*).

As the former debt is extinguished, novation has been classed amongst the causes of extinction of obligations. Mourlon says that *novation* is both *productive* and *extinctive* of obligations, and should therefore rank amongst the means of extinguishing obligations. Therein Mourlon contradicts his own remarks upon the resolutive condition, which he criticised as being in its wrong place amongst the means of extinction. The reader will remember that I refused to accept Mourlon's theory with regard to the resolutive condition, and here, on novation, I find him contradicting his former remarks, and proving that we would be right in rejecting his opinion upon the resolutive condition.

The *will* to form a novation must exist or else it cannot take place (*b*).

In consequence, only those to whom we can pay effectively can cause novation; it follows that a minor, a woman under her husband's authority, interdicted persons, etc., cannot cause novation (*c*).

A tutor or curator or husband can make a novation; even Vénulius says that a joint and several creditor can make novation (*d*).

Novation made by the substitution of a new debtor,

(*a*) Poth. Ob. 581.
(*b*) *Idem*, 582.
(*c*) *Idem*, 590; 1. 3; 1. 20, sec. 1, ff. d. tit.: *Cui recte solvitur is etiam novare potest*: 1. 10, ff. de novat.
(*d*) Poth. Ob. 592.

may be made between the creditor and the new debtor, without the intervention of the old debtor, or without his knowledge (*a*).

The former debt is extinguished the same as if payment had taken place : such is the effect of novation.

Delegation is a kind of novation whereby the former debtor, to clear himself, towards his creditor, offers a third party, who taking his place, is bound towards the creditor (*b*).

In this the concurrence of three and often four persons is necessary—1st. The delegating party. 2nd. The one delegated. 3rd. The creditor and sometimes—4th. A person whom the creditor indicated and towards whom the one delegated is obliged.

If the one delegated is obliged only under condition—all effect of the delegation is suspended until the condition is fulfilled (*c*).

If the one delegated be obliged truly towards the creditor to whom he is delegated, the delegating party is fully free from that creditor and the creditor has no recourse against him, even though the new debtor become insolvent. The creditor in accepting the delegation followed the solvency of the debtor delegated to him (*d*).

(*a*) *Idem*, 598 : *Liberat me is qui quod debeo promittit, etamsi nolim ;* l. 8, sec. 5, ff. de novat.

(*b*) Poth. Ob. 600: *Delegare est vice suâ alium reum dare creditori, vel sui jusserit* ; l. 11, ff. de novat.

(*c*) Poth. Ob. 603.

(*d*) *Idem*, 604: *nomen ejus secutus est*.

Delegation, transfer and indication differ from each other, and all differ from novation. The *transfer* that a creditor makes of a claim is not *novation*, it is the same claim still; the *indication* of a person from whom to receive payment is a mere *mandate* and not a *novation*; no new debt arises therefrom (a).

As we have seen, there are three modes of causing novation—1st. By change of the object. 2nd. By change of the *debtor*. 3rd. By change of the *creditor*. 1st. When the creditor and debtor agree that one thing shall be paid in place of another. 2nd. When a third party frees the debtor by paying for him. 3rd. When the debtor is freed from the creditor by means of another party that the creditor has offered him. In case No. 2, the consent of two parties suffices, but in case No. 3, the consent of three persons is necessary (b).

In ancient Roman law, novation was *presumed*, but under Justinian it had to be *expressed*. The Code Napoleon takes a mid-way. It is not presumed, but it need not, of necessity, be expressed. The will suffices (c).

We may conclude then—1st. That a debt that is *null* cannot be novated. 2nd. That a *good* debt cannot be novated by one that is *null*. 3rd. That a debt *annulable* may be novated by a *good* and *valid* debt. 4th. Can the *good* and *valid* debt be novated by one

---

(a) Poth. Ob. 605.
(b) Maur. vol. ii. Nos. 1396 to 1402.
(c) *Idem*, No. 1404.

that is *annulable?* 5th. Can a *conditional* debt be novated by a *pure* and *simple* one? 6th. Can a *pure* and *simple* debt be novated by a *conditional* one? (*a*).

En resumé.—1st case.—When the debt to be novated is *null*, the new obligation cannot arise, having no ground whereon to rest.

2nd case.—When the new debt is *null*, the extinction of the old one does not take place, there being no power in the new one to extinguish it.

3rd case.—All obligations liable to be validly paid, may be validly novated. (There is an exception for gaming debts.)

4th case.—When the old debt is valid and the new one annulable, the former revives if the latter is annulled.

5th case.—If the old debt was conditional, the new one can exist only in as much as the condition of the old one has been fulfilled.

6th case.—When the old debt is pure and simple, and the new one conditional, the new one exists and the old is extinguished only in as much as the condition, to which the new one is subject, has been fulfilled (*b*).

As a principle, the old debt, being extinguished, its accessories go with it.

Pothier says: "When the novation takes place by the substitution of a new debtor to the old one, the hypo-

---

(*a*) *Idem*, Nos. 1405, etc.

(*b*) *Idem*, No. 1410; Aubry et Rau, vol. iv. sec. 324, notes 18 to 24; sec. 324, note 12; Dur. vol. xii. Nos. 296, 300; Demolombe, vol. v. Nos. 248, 253, etc.; Marcadé, art. 1272.

thecs that covered the goods of the former debtor cannot be continued without his consent." Mourlon don't like this, but he says the Code sanctions it (a).

There are two kinds of delegation—1st. Perfect. 2nd. Imperfect.

1st. Perfect delegation, is a convention whereby a debtor frees himself, by giving in his place a person whom the creditor accepts as debtor. The article of the Code Napoleon would lead us to think that it should be expressed. Duranton says it ought to be admitted when it results clearly from the circumstances; so thinks Pothier. Mourlon cannot accept their opinions as the article of the Code Napoléon is too formal (b).

(Our article 1173, does not say it should be expressed, but it leads one to reject, both the opinions of Duranton and Pothier, for it says : "Unless it is evident that the creditor intends to discharge the debtor who makes the delegation." Now it cannot be *evident* unless it is expressed in some way.)

2nd. Imperfect delegation, is one that contains no novation. It takes place when the creditor who accepted the new debtor does not discharge the former debtor. In *perfect* delegation the creditor receives a new debtor in place of a former one; in *imperfect* delegation, the new debtor does not replace the former one, but becomes his co-debtor (c).

(a) Mour. vol. ii. 1415.
(b) *Idem*, No. 1417.
(c) *Idem*, No. 1420.

Section IV.—*Of Release.*

"The release of an obligation may be made either expressly or tacitly by persons legally capable of alienating. It is made tacitly when the creditor voluntarily surrenders to his debtor the original title of the obligation, unless there is proof of a contrary intention." "The surrender of a thing given in pledge does not create a presumption of the release of the debt for which it was pledged" (*a*). The surrender of the title to a joint and several debtor avails his co-debtors. An express release to one of the joint and several debtors does not discharge the others. If granted to a principal debtor it discharges the sureties, but not *vice versa*. Nor if granted to one surety does it discharge the others.

New Law.—["That which the creditor receives from a surety as a consideration for releasing him from his suretyship is not imputed in discharge of the principal debtor, or of the other sureties, except as regards the latter, in cases in which they have a recourse upon the one released, and to the extent of such recourse"] (*b*).

The release of the debt may be made, not only by a special express convention; but also by a tacit one (*c*).

(*a*) Arts. 1181 to 1187.
(*b*) Art. 1186.
(*c*) Poth. Ob. 608: *si debitoris meo reddiderim cautionem videtur inter nos convenisse nepeteram*; l. 2, sec. 1, ff. de pact.

Does the possession of the note, by the debtor, cause a presumption that the debt is released? Boiceau distinguishes between the cases where the debtor claims to have paid the debt, and when he claims that the debt is forgiven by the creditor. Our Code makes no such distinction (*a*).

Restitution by the creditor to the debtor of the object held in guarantee does not indicate that the debt is forgiven; it merely shows the creditor's confidence in the debtor's solvency (*b*).

Real release is when the debtor declares the debt released or gives a receipt therefor (*c*).

Personal release is where the creditor merely declares the debtor free from any personal obligation (*d*).

Here arises a very widely disputed question. If I receive a sum from a surety to free him, can I afterwards demand the whole debt from the debtor? Dumoulin says, yes. Because I am only paid by the surety to free him, and it is presumed that what he pays me is not worth more to him than his freedom. He prefers to pay so much than to risk the solvency of the debtor. *Nemo res suas jacture facilè præsumi-*

(*a*) Poth. Ob. 609.
(*b*) *Idem*, 610.
(*c*) *Idem*, 616.
(*d*) *Idem*, 617. This release *magis eximit personam debitoris ab obligatione quàm extinguit obligationem.*

tur. (Our Code agrees with this, but the Code Napoleon does not) (*a*).

A tutor, curator, etc., have no power to release a debt belonging to those under their care (*b*).

The law 2. sec. 1 ff. *de pact*, presumes a debt to be released when the creditor restores the note of hand or other note to the debtor; but as it is not a presumption *juris et de jure*, it does not exclude the creditor from proving that the debt is not paid (*c*).

From the principle that the release is *au fonds*—a gratuitous act, it results—1st. That it can only be done by one capable of disposing gratuitously. 2nd. It must be made to a debtor capable of receiving by gratuitous title. 3rd. It is *restorable* if the debtor succeeds his former creditor. 4th. It is *reducible* if it exceeds the disposable amount. 5th. It is *revocable* for ingratitude, or appearance of children (*d*).

Release is *real* when absolute, general and under no restriction; it is *personal* when it is limited to such and such a person. Tacit release, that is the abandonment of the title, is always *real;* for a creditor who had no intention of releasing the debt would naturally keep the title to it.

1st. The release of the title to one of the joint and several debtors, frees the others. 2nd. When several

---

(*a*) Poth. Ob. 618; C. C. L. C. art. 1186: *nemo res suas jactare facilè præsumitur*.

(*b*) Poth. Ob. 619, lex 37, ff. de pact.

(*c*) Poth. Ob. 847.

(*d*) Mour. vol. ii. No. 1422.

persons contract jointly the same debt, by the same deed, (but not jointly and severally), the release of the title to one frees the others. 3rd. The release of the title to one of the sureties benefits the others. 4th. Consequently the release to a debtor clears all the sureties (*a*).

The Code Napoleon says that whatever a creditor received from a surety *to discharge him from his suretyship* should be imputed on the debt of the principal or the other sureties. This would be avoided by merely omitting to mention the amount in the release. A law so open to violation is not a good law. Our Code, art. 1186, new law, is the contrary of this, and our article is most reasonable (*b*).

Section V.—*Of Compensation.*

"When two persons are mutually debtor and creditor of each other, both debts are extinguished by compensation which takes place between them in the cases and manner hereinafter declared" (*c*).

Compensation exists by law between two debts equally liquidated and demandable, each for a sum of

(*a*) *Idem*, No. 1432.
(*b*) *Idem*, No. 1437; Bug. sur Poth. vol. ii. p. 330; C. C. L. C. 1186.
(*c*) Arts. 1187 to 1198.

money, or equal quantity of a determined thing, and from the moment of their co-existence. "It is not prevented by a term granted by indulgence for the payment of one of the debts."

"Compensation takes place whatever be the cause or consideration of the debts or of either of them, except in the following cases—1st. The demand in restitution of a thing of which the owner has been unjustly deprived. 2nd. The demand in restitution of a deposit. 3rd. A debt which has for object an alimentary provision not liable to seizure " (a).

The surety may avail himself of compensation when the creditor owes the principal debtor. But the debtor cannot claim it for the debt his creditor owes the surety. A joint and several debtor cannot set up the debt the creditor owes his co-debtor. Debtor cannot set up against the assignee the compensation he could have set up against the assignor. When two debts are payable at different places, compensation cannot be set up unless the expenses of remittance be paid. When compensation by law is prevented by any cause, the party in whose favour it is prevented may demand it by exception. When there are several debts the rules of imputation of payment apply.

"Compensation does not take place to the prejudice of the rights acquired by third parties " (b).

"He who pays a debt which is of right extinguished by compensation cannot afterwards, in enforcing the

(a) Art. 1190.
(b) Art. 1196.

debt which he has failed to set up in compensation, avail himself, to the prejudice of third parties, of the privileges and hypothecs attached to such debt, unless there were just grounds for his ignorance of its existence at the time of payment" (a).

Compensation is known in Ontario and elsewhere by the more familiar term of—*Off-set.*

Compensation is the extinction of two debts contracted between two parties reciprocally and co-existant (b).

Pomponius shows how it is a mutual interest to compensate (c).

A creditor is obliged to compensate to the amount of his debtor's claim, even though it be less than his own claim (d).

Compensation may be opposed in all cases wherein the objects are susceptible thereof. *For example,* a sum of money, or other divisible objects, as hay, oats, wine, etc. (e).

The two objects must be of the same kind (f).

The debt opposed in compensation must be due (g).

(a) Art. 1197.
(b) Poth. Ob. 623: *Compensatio est debiti et crediti inter se contributio;* 1. i, ff. de compens.
(c) Pomponius shows it to be a mutual interest.
(d) Poth. Ob. 538.
(e) *Idem,* 624.
(f) *Idem,* 626: *Compensatio debiti ex pari specie, licet ex causâ dispari, admittitur;* Paul. sent. ii. v. 3.
(g) Poth. Ob. 627: *Quod in diem debetur, non compensabitur antiquam dies veniat;* 1. 7, ff. de compens.

The debt must be demandable; a contested debt cannot be the object of compensation (a).

It takes place *deplein droit*, that is by law solely without necessity of being expressed (b).

Payment made by one debtor frees the other. I have two debtors, John and Thomas. They owe me $1,000. I become John's debtor for $1,000. Does Thomas' debt to me become compensated? Papinien say, no; Domat says, yes (c).

If my creditor for $100 becomes my debtor for $100 and I have paid him, I can recover the amount by action, *condictio indebiti* (d).

Compensation is based on a motive of public use and a motive of justice.

There are three conditions—1st. The two debts should have for objects sums of money, or things of the same kind that are indeterminate. 2nd. The two debts must be liquidated. 3rd. Be demandable. The first condition demands no explanation. In the second case a debt is liquidated when it is known to be due and the amount is known; *cum certum est an et quantum debeatur*. In the third case there are several points—1st. A term of grace does not form an obstacle to the compensation. 2nd. Debts of a debtor who has failed, although they become demandable by

---

(a) Poth. Ob. 628.

(b) *Idem*, 635; *Placuit id quod invicem debetur* Ipso Jure compensari; l. 21, ff. de comp.

(c) Poth. Ob. 274.

(d) *Idem*, 639; Ulpien in legem 10, sec. 1, ff. de comp.

the fact of his failure, are not allowed to compensate debts due him and demandable (*a*).

The above being the rules it follows—1st. That it is not necessary that the two debts be known to the parties. 2nd. Nor that they be of equal value. 3rd. Nor that they be payable at the same place. 4th. Nor that they spring from the same cause (*b*).

Though a debt springing from a sale may be compensated by one coming from a lease, etc., etc., still there are four exceptions to this—1st. Of a debt whose object consists in something declared non-subject to seizure. 2nd. The demand in restitution of something of which the owner was unjustly deprived. 3rd. The demand in restitution of a deposit. 4th. The demand in restitution of a loan (*c*).

The principle that compensation may arise, even without the knowledge of the parties, entails several consequences—1st. The incapacity of the parties is no obstacle to compensation. 2nd. The interest ceases to run from the moment of the co-existence of the debt. 3rd. From that instant the accessories, privileges, etc., are extinguished. Can it take place in spite of a co-debtor? (*d*).

(*a*) Mour. vol. ii. Nos. 1439 to 1444. See Traité de droit Commercial, by M. M. Bravard and Demangeat, vol. v. p. 154, etc.

(*b*) Mour. vol. ii. No. 1444.

(*c*) See Marcadé, art. 1293; Aubry and Rau, vol. iv. sec. 327; Demol. vol. v. Nos. 598, 599.

(*d*) In Roman law, compensation had to be pleaded. See Mourlon, vol. ii. No. 1452.

The surety may set up compensation in favour of the principal debtor when he neglects to do so himself (*a*).

Optional compensation is one declared by the judge or alleged by the party. It can only be set up by the one in whose favour the law acts. I deposit $500 with you. I subsequently become heir of a man to whom you owe that amount. You cannot demand compensation, because it is a debt springing from a deposit, but I can demand it (*b*).

SECTION VI—*Of Confusion.*

"When the qualities of the creditor and debtor are united in the same person, there arises a confusion which extinguishes the obligation; nevertheless, in certain cases when confusion ceases to exist, its effects cease also" (*c*).

"The confusion which takes place by the concurrence of the qualities of creditor and principal debtor in the same person avails the sureties. That which takes place by the concurrence of the qualities of surety and

---

(*a*) If possible, get this work, and read 1452, pages 771, etc.; Aubry et Rau, vol. iv. sec. 326.

(*b*) Mour. vol. ii. No. 1460.

(*c*) Arts. 1198 to 1200.

creditor or of surety and principal debtor, does not extinguish the principal obligation" (*a*).

Confusion takes place when the creditor becomes heir to the debtor or *vice versa* (*b*).

It entails extinction of the sureties (*c*).

Extinction of debt does not follow from confusion of the sureties (*d*).

Confusion has no effect upon third parties who have an interest in the debt, nor when there are several debtors and only one becomes creditor. The others are still liable for their shares (*e*).

It is revoked, when its causes cease to exist, *v.g.*, a revoked will creating the debtor heir, etc.

It ceases, when by a new event its cause has disappeared, *v.g.*, the debtor who succeeded his creditor sells out to a third party; the claim is only paralyzed but not extinguished. It revives (*f*).

Frain, in his *Recueil d'Arrêts du Parlement de Bretagne*, in the report of 12th January, 1621, says: A penal obligation added to a promise for another is valid, although we cannot validly promise for another. *Non de alio, sed de se.* The example he gives is pecu-

(*a*) Art. 1199.
(*b*) Poth. Ob. 642: *non potest esse obligatio sine personâ obligatâ*.
(*c*) L. 38, sec. 1, ff. de fidej.; Poth Ob. 644.
(*d*) Poth. Ob. 645; l. 71, ff. de fidejussor: *si creditor fidejussor jussori hæres, fuerit, vel fidejussor creditori, puto convenire confussione obligationis, non liberari reum*.
(*e*) Mour. vol. ii. page 775, etc.
(*f*) *Idem*, page 800.

liar. The father of a canon of the church, who had offended the bishop of St. Malo, promised the bishop that his son, the canon, would not show his face in the city of St. Malo for the space of four months. And he bound himself to pay, in case his son, the canon, should break the agreement, the sum of £300. The canon broke the agreement and the father was condemned to pay the sum. Although of no interest, strictly speaking, I may add that the canon wore a mask and thereby *did not show his face.* One day the mask fell off, and in consequence the father was punished for his trick and rash promise.

SECTION VII—*Performance of Obligation becoming impossible.*

" When the certain specific thing which is the object of an obligation perishes, or the delivery of it becomes from any other cause impossible, without any act or fault of the debtor, and before he is in default, the obligation is extinguished ; it is also extinguished although the debtor be in default, if the thing would equally have perished in the possession of the creditor ; unless in either of the above mentioned cases the debtor has expressly bound himself for fortuitous events. The debtor must prove the fortuitous event which he alleges. The destruction of a thing stolen or the impossibility of delivering it, does not discharge him who stole the thing, or him who knowingly received it, from the obligation to pay its value" (*a*).

When the performance becomes impossible, without any fault of the debtor, he is bound to assign to the creditor such rights of indemnity as he may possess.

"When the performance of an obligation to do has become impossible without any act or fault of the debtor and before he is in default, the obligation is extinguished and both parties are liberated; but if the obligation be beneficially performed in part, the creditor is bound to the extent of the benefit actually received by him" (*b*).

There can be no debt without an object due; the extinction of that object naturally extinguishes the debt (*c*).

For the same reason if the thing due becomes unsusceptible of being the object of an obligation, the debt becomes extinguished (*d*).

An object lost so as that its discovery is not possible, is almost the same as if it were destroyed; there being no fault on the debtor's part (*e*).

In case of alternative obligations, the loss of one of the objects does not extinguish the debt with regard to the other (*f.*)

(*a*) Arts. 1200 to 1202, inclusively.
(*b*) Art. 1202.
(*c*) Poth. Ob. 649. lex. 33, 57, ff. de Verb. Oblig.
(*d*) Poth. Ob. 650: *Is qui alienum servum promisit, perducto ea ad libertatem, non tenetur;* l. 51, ff. de Verb. Oblig.
(*e*) Poth. Ob. 656.
(*f*) Poth. Ob. 657.

When the debtor, by a special clause, binds himself for all the risks, etc., of the object, there is an exception to the rule (*a*).

Three cases of loss may arise—1st. Total destruction of the object. 2nd. Its becoming non-commercial, as the case of land taken for railway purposes. 3rd. When so lost that its whereabouts is completely ignored, as in the case it were stolen (*b*).

The robber is in default by the fact of his robbery. When it is lost, but not through any fault of the debtor, he is not responsible, but—1st. He must give up all its accessories and privileges. 2nd. He must restore what is left of it, if any. 3rd. He must transfer to the creditor all actions, etc. (*c*).

No one is held to the impossible. Loss of the thing due, is too narrow a maxim, we should add, that the arising of an event that renders the accomplishment of the obligation impossible, is a sufficient cause of extinction (*d*).

(*a*) *Idem*, 668.
(*b*) Mour. vol. ii. No. 1467.
(*c*) *Idem*, No. 1479.
(*d*) *Idem*, No. 1480; Aubry et Rau, vol. iv. sec. 331; Demol. vol. v. No. 786. See in the Code Napoléon, arts. 1138, 1719, No. 3, 1722, 1741, and finally 1795 and 1791, and the C. C. L. C. arts. 1025, 1612, No. 3 (the words *to give*, should be *to procure for*), 1660, 1659, and finally 1692 and 1687.

CHAPTER XII.

ON PROOF.

Besides the modes of extinction of obligations that our Code has thus far treated of, there are other means, which I style extraordinary means of extinction. They are scattered here and there throughout the Code, and do not come within the range of this essay. There are still fifty-four articles, upon proof, testimony, presumptions, admissions, oaths of parties, decisory oath, and oath put officially, which the codifiers have given us under the title of Obligations. To say the least, I do not think that these subjects should be included in this title. I fancy that proof is of a character sufficiently distinctive to merit being classed under a title for itself. Moreover, does it not savour very much of Procedure?

For these and other reasons, I have concluded not to include in this Essay the chapter on Proof. It is sufficiently important to demand a full Essay, even as large as this, for itself, while the principal readers of this sketch—that is the laymen—would find it merely an obstacle, bringing with it too much matter and of too varied a kind to be easily grasped at once.

Still, I deem it not out of place to give a very general idea of the rules that govern the Proof and Testimony before the Courts. In the next chapter, I shall resume all that has been said about obligations, and in a few pages give a synopsis of the matter, in such a way that, with the map in Chapter III. and this synopsis, the reader shall have a compendium of the whole, while for details he can look up the index and find them in the body of this Essay.

"The party who claims the performance of an obligation must prove it. On the other hand, he who alleges facts in avoidance or extinction of the obligation must prove them" (*a*).

"The proof produced must be the best of which the case in its nature is susceptible. Secondary or inferior proof cannot be received unless it is first shown that the best or primary proof cannot be produced" (*b*).

"Proof may be made by writings, by testimony, by presumptions, by the confession of the party, or by his oath, according to the rules declared in this chapter, and in the manner provided in the Code of Procedure" (*c*).

Thus the primary proof must be written, and until it is shown that it cannot be obtained, other or secondary proof is not admissible. There are degrees also in the writings which may be classed amongst the

(*a*) Art. 1203.
(*b*) Art. 1204.
(*c*) Art. 1205.

means of written proof. Firstly, we have *authentic writings.* These are the very best proof. Records, etc., of governments, minutes, etc., of councils (county or municipal); notarial documents, signed by a notary and all the parties. Witnesses to these, whenever necessary, must be twenty-one years of age. But aliens may be witnesses.

Next come copies of authentic writings; extracts, duly signed and attested by a prothonotary of the Superior Court; copies of originals, signed by the notary who drew up the originals.

Next come official documents made outside of Lower Canada. They make *prima facie* evidence, without it being necessary to prove the authenticity of the seal, signature, etc.

After these, private writings make best proof. Family registers and papers do not make proof in favour of him by whom they are written; in case they formally declare a payment received, or when they express that a minute is made to supply a defect of title. What is written by a creditor on the back of any title or deed he holds, although he may not have signed it, is proof against him.

Then, where there are no writings, authentic, copy, or private, proof must be made by testimony. It was an old maxim in Roman law, that one witness was no witness—*testis unus, testis nullus;* but our law completely destroys it. "The testimony of one witness

OF ADMISSIONS. 143

is sufficient in all cases in which proof by testimony is admitted" (*a*).

"All persons are legally competent to give testimony, except—1st. Persons deficient in understanding, whether from immaturity of age, insanity or other cause. 2nd. Those insensible to the religious obligations of an oath. 3rd. Those civilly dead. 4th. Those declared infamous by law. 5th. Husband and wife, for or against each other" (*b*).

Testimony cannot be given in one's own favour.

Presumptions are those which arise from law, and those which arise from fact. As to the former, there is no permission to contradict them by proof, unless the law pointedly reserves that right for a party. The authority of a final judgment (*res judicata*) is a presumption *juris et de jure*. Presumptions not established by law are left to the discretion of the court.

Admissions may be judicial or extra-judicial. The former are complete proof against the party making them; the latter must be proved by writing or the oath of the party against whom they are set up.

To complete imperfect proof the court may examine a party to the suit upon oath. Or, again, the party may be thus examined upon interrogatories on articulated facts, or by decisory oath.

The decisory oath may be offered by either of the parties to the other. He to whom the oath is offered,

(*a*) Art. 1230.
(*b*) Art. 1231.

and refuses to take it or to refer it to his adversary, fails in his demand or exception. So for the adversary to whom he referred it, and who refused to take it. But the moment the oath is accepted and the statement made upon it, the one who offered or referred the oath is not permitted to contradict the statement.

"The oath put officially by the court to one of the parties cannot be referred by him to the other. The oath, upon the value of the thing demanded, can only be put by the court officially to the party claiming, when it is impossible to establish such value otherwise" (a).

It will be seen, by the foregoing sketch, that this Chapter of Proof has a special interest for lawyers, and that it belongs, somewhat, to the domain of Procedure. I do not see the necessity of any more upon the subject, in this Essay.

(a) Arts. 1255 and 1256.

CHAPTER XIII.

A SYNOPSIS OF OBLIGATIONS.

Let me draw the attention of the reader to the map —chapter III—and with it before the eye, we shall proceed to give, in a few short pages, the sum and substance of all that has been gleaned from Latin and French authors, from the Code Napolèon and our Civil Code of Lower Canada, and expressed in the foregoing chapters, from III. to XII.

Once more recall that species of syllogism wherein I expressed the way of learning when there is a right to an action at law, and when there is no such right.

Two things are necessary in order that an *action at law* may be had—1st. The *existence* of an obligation; and 2nd. The *violation* of that obligation. It is therefore necessary to know four things—1st. What is an obligation. 2nd. Whence an obligation arises. 3rd. How many kinds of obligations may exist; and 4th. How an obligation becomes extinguished.

While the first three questions are being examined there may be a violation of the obligation, that will give rise to an action at law; but the moment the fourth question comes up and any of the means of extinction of obligations arises, there is no power or right to such action any more. But it is well to know when an obligation is extinguished—also how violated.

Then let us answer rapidly the four questions— I. What is an obligation? II. What are the sources of obligations? III. How many kinds are there of of obligations? IV. How is an obligation extinguished?

I. *What is an obligation?* An obligation is a legal tie by which one person is bound towards another to give, to do, or not to do something.

II. *What are the sources of obligations?* They are five in number—1st. Contracts. 2nd. Quasi-contracts. 3rd. Offences. 4th. Quasi-offences. 5th. The sole operation of the Law.

Let us examine each of these—without one of these five there is no obligation—if no obligation there can be no violation of one, and if no violation of one, there can be no *action at law*.

1st. *Contracts.* A contract is a convention whereby two parties reciprocally, or one of them only, promises and binds himself to give, to do or not to do something. There are four causes of nullity of contracts— error, fraud, violence, and lesion. The error must be in something material to the contract; the fraud must be of a nature that the party would not have contracted had it not been for it; the violence and fear must be, the one sufficiently dangerous and the other sufficiently grave; lesion must be against minors and of sufficient consequence.

2nd. *A quasi-contract* : is the lawful and voluntary act of a person whereby he binds another towards him, or himself towards another, without the intervention of any contract between them. As in the case of one who undertakes the management of an absentee's estate.

3rd. *An offence,* and 4th. *A quasi-offence:* are the actions of a person, capable of discerning right from wrong, and who by his fault, imprudence, neglect or want of skill causes a damage to another. The offence is when he is the actor himself; the quasi-offence when it is his servant, child, horse, or any one or anything under his care.

5th. *The sole operation of the law* is a source of obligations in such cases as that of children obliged to provide for indigent parents.

These are the sources of obligations. From these five sources and only from these can an obligation arise. And once it exists it has a suspensive effect until either its extinction or its violation. In the first case, things go back to their position anterior to the existence of the obligation, and in the second case an action at law arises.

III. *How many kinds of obligations ?* There are six divisions upon this question—1st. Conditional obligations. 2nd. Obligations with a term. 3rd. Alternative obligations. 4th. Joint and several obligations. 5th. Divisible and indivisible obligations. 6th. Obligations with a penal clause. Each of these six points will bear a definition.

1st. *A conditional obligation* is one made to depend upon an event future and uncertain, either by suspending it until the event happens, or by dissolving it accordingly as the event does or does not happen.

2nd. *An obligation with a term* differs from the suspensive condition inasmuch as it does not suspend the obligation, but only delays the execution of it.

3rd. *An alternative obligation* is one wherein the debtor is discharged by giving or doing one of the two things which form the object of the obligation.

4th. *Joint and several obligations*, as far as creditors go, give to each of them singly the right of exacting the performance of the whole obligation and thereupon discharging the debtor; and as far as debtors go, that bind the co-debtors all for the same thing, in such a manner that each of them singly may be compelled to the performance of the whole obligation, and that the performance by one discharges the others towards the creditor.

5th. *Divisible obligations* are those that have for their objects, things which in their delivery or performance are susceptible of division either materially or intellectually. The *indivisible obligations* are the contrary.

6th. *The penal clause* is a secondary obligation by which a person, to assure the performance of the primary obligation, binds himself to a penalty in case of its inexecution.

These then are the six classes of obligations that may arise from any of the five sources before mentioned. At this point they are either *violated* or become *extinguished.* If violated, the courts are prepared to hear the dispute and remedy the wrong; if not violated, in the course of nature they become extinguished.

IV. *How are obligations extinguished?* By six ordinary means and by six extraordinary means—1st. Payment. 2nd. Novation. 3rd. Release. 4th. Compensation. 5th. Confusion. 6th. Performance becoming impossible. Let us define each of these.

1st. *Payment* is not only the delivery of a sum of money, but the performance of anything to which the parties are respectively obliged.

2nd. *Novation* is the substituting one debt for another either by change of the object, by change of the debtor, or by change of the creditor.

3rd. *Release* is the surrender, express or tacit, by a creditor to his right or claim upon the debtor.

4th. *Compensation*—known as off-set—is the becoming of two parties mutually debtor and creditor of each other.

5th. *Confusion* is the blending of the qualities of debtor and creditor in the same person.

6th. *Performance becoming impossible,* may be the total loss of the object or its delivery becoming impossible. This is a mode of extinction of obligations only when there is no fault on the part of the debtor.

Now we turn to the six extraordinary means of extinction of obligations, they need merely be named and require no further notice—1st. Judgment in nullity. 2nd. Resolutive condition. 3rd. Prescription. 4th. Expiration of time limited by law. 5th. Death of the creditor or of the debtor. 6th. By special clauses applicable to special contracts.

In these few pages the reader has a *resumé* of all that may be found in the whole essay. Now that you know what an obligation is, how many kinds of them exist and whence they spring, you have a pretty good idea whether you have contracted any obligation towards anyone or not. If you have, you know now how that obligation may be extinguished, and you can tell whether such extinction has taken place or not. If not, has the obligation been violated or not? By your answer to this question you know whether you have a right to an action at law, or whether any person has a right to one against you or not. Knowing these things, you are safe, and the details belong to the lawyers.

The questions of procedure and proof are for the members of the Bar alone, while the general questions of obligations are not only for them and the students, but also for all citizens of this Dominion.

I have striven in this essay to fulfil my promises. I give a plan of the whole Code, then a map of obligations, followed by all the details of that important title,—not my own arbitrary expressions, but the translated statements of the most eminent jurists and renowned authorities; then the full list of those authorities, at the bottom of each page, their names, the volume, page or number of each work. Having gone through the title from end to end, I subjoin a short chapter on proof and, in this present chapter, give the synopsis of the whole essay, which is, in itself, but a feeble synopsis of a gigantic subject.

The only object I have in view is the imparting of useful information to the public. I have had many a long hunt, through the wilderness of old ideas and new opinions, for the subject matter of these few pages, and I now place at the disposal of my fellow-countrymen the spoils of that chase.

CHAPTER XIV.

CONCLUSION.

The study of the law is far from being a dry one; combining the knowledge of many sciences, it is likewise rich in literature and lofty prose. It has a history as well as a philosophy peculiar to itself. By no means can I better illustrate the depth, the beauty, and the utility of such a study, than by taking one example, a single phrase in the laws of the Romans, and tracing it, as you follow a stream from its source to the sea, from its first appearance amongst the laws of the Romans, down along the ages, now meandering slowly along, now leaping from the cliffs of time, here gleaming out in the sunshine, there hidden, for a space, beneath the earth, through all its vicissitudes until, at last, it flows calmly into the broad sea of our codified system.

Opening the ancient laws at random, I find—"*Si ita stipulatus fuero decem aut quinque dari spondes, quinque debentur.*" *Law 12th on obligations.* "Thus if you promise to give ten or five *séstertii*, five you shall owe and not ten." The principle is, when two things are stipulated and the disjunctive (or) is used, that the party stipulating is only bound to one, and that the lesser of the two. This law has been laid down by the first Roman legislators before the days of the Empire.

The first question that you may ask, is, what are *séstertii?* It is the plural of *séstertius*, a Roman coin. Among them the computation was by SESTERTII NUMMI as follows:

	l.	s.	d.	q.
A sestertius equals............	0	0	0	1¾
10 sestertii equal.	0	1	7	1½
1000 sestertii equal.				
A sestertium equals..........	8	1	5	2
10 sestertia equal	80	14	7	0
100 sestertia equal...........	807	5	10	0

But you say this is numismatics. Most assuredly it is; from the Roman term nummus we get the name, and you see how I can, if I desire, unite the study of numismatics with that of the law. I merely give the above by way of illustration, that the reader may see how, in the true study of the law, we require the study of other sciences. Let us take up our law 12 of the ancient Romans, and follow it for awhile. We need not go back to the days of the kings, or to the time of the consuls, for this special law did not then exist. We cannot trace it, as we may many others to the Tribunes or the laws of the twelve tables. The orders of consuls, the opinions of jurists, the edicts of the prætors and commands of emperors seem to have constituted the legal guides until we come to the days of Constantine the Great.

Thirty-one years, from A.D. 306 to A.D. 337, this famous monarch held sway. But only from A.D. 325 had he sole title of Emperor. When, at the death of Maxeminus he was elected Emperor, the army made choice of Maxentius. Constantine offered him most favourable terms, but he refused them; thence sprung the quarrel, which was settled on the field of battle. The cross was flung out, a glorious supernatural standard upon the sky, and in the name of the God of the Christian, Constantine marched to victory.

The Empire was divided into east and west. The phantom of an Empire hovered over the east; and the west, ravaged by the barbaric hordes of the north, tottered to its fall.

But if ruin seized upon the monuments of ancient Rome, and the ubiquity of her mighty dominion was curtailed, yet her laws lived, and despite the ravages of the Huns and the approaching desolation of that giant of the past, those laws were preserved and embodied in Codes and Institutes.

Pre-eminent in history as the first Christian emperor, famous as a conqueror, yet Constantine, in 325, caused his Constitution to be written which perpetuated for one hundred and fifty years those laws, which Justinian was destined to embalm for the guidance and use of untold generations.

Like Constantine, Justinian was a conqueror; but he gave to the world the model of future legislation in his Digest of the Laws, the Pandects, the famous Institutes, to which A.D. 534, he added his memorable Code. During his life, there were only the Digest, Institutes and Code; but after his death, which took place in 566, his own constitutions were collected and called the *Novellæ* or Novels of Justinian.

For three hundred years after his death, the body of laws compiled by Justinian was observed in the east. Even in his own day, the Code and Digest were translated into Greek.

In the west, the bodies of laws compiled by this famous emperor, had at first only effect in the western provinces of Italy. The rest of the west being under the barbaric laws of the Goths, Huns, Vandals, Lombards and Franks. Despite these ravages, Ravenna conserved vestiges of the Roman laws. In Gaul, there existed a strange mixture of Roman and French laws. Alaric, second king of the Goths, seeing that the Gauls detested the Gothic laws, had, in 506, a Code of Roman laws compiled and published, under the name of Theodosian Code, for their benefit.

Behold that beautiful picture, drawn by one of our

greatest modern writers, of the fall of Roman splendour and the approach of that long night of barbarism and division that was about to settle upon Europe!

"Poor Boëthius," writes Bulwer, "rich, nobly born, a consul, his sons consuls—the world one smile to the last philosopher of Rome. Then suddenly, against this type of the old world's departing *wisdom*, stands frowning the new world's grim genius *force*. Theodoric the Ostrogoth condemning Boëthius, the schoolman, and Boëthius in his Pavan dungeon, holding a dialogue with the shade of Athenian Philosophy. It is the finest picture upon which lingers the glimmering of the western golden day, before night rushes over time."

And the night came. Monuments were levelled, libraries destroyed, civilization bleeding and crushed, cried for mercy; yet beneath the lava tide, gorgeous and perfect as the mosaics of Pompeii or the marble columns of Herculaneum, reposed those pillars and checker-work of ancient legislation—buried in the volcanic eruptions of the north, buried to be again disinterred, in years to come, beautiful and perfect as ever—even the shattered fragments the more precious for their antiquity, olden grace, and pristine splendour.

Charlemagne, that great politician and warrior, being crowned Emperor of the West, A.D. 800, overthrew the power of the Lombards and abolished their laws. He revived the Roman laws; but his success was not great, for even three hundred years later on, in 1100, the body of Roman laws, compiled by Justinian, was unknown in the west, and Alaric's Code was only followed in a few provinces.

Lothaire II. brought back the ancient grandeur of the days of Justinian by reviving his law, while Frederick I. promised to aid in that great undertaking. Frederick II., his grandson, who was elected Emperor in 1212, paid special attention to and conferred favours on all who cultivated the science of the laws. He united to the Code of Justinian several chapters of a new Code.

An old author on Roman and Ancient laws, M. Claude-Joseph de Ferriere, says: "Behold the destiny of the Roman laws! It seems that Divine Providence, in destroying so vast and so flourishing an Empire, wished, for the good of the people, to conserve that perfect model of jurisprudence. We can never too much admire the wisdom of God, who, in overthrowing the throne of the Emperors, preserved, in all Europe, the empire of their laws. Thus, people who suffered under their yoke have freely recognized their laws, while people, who were never conquered by the arms of the Romans, have accepted the authority and power of Roman jurisprudence."

The Roman laws spread over Europe, and France, more than any other country, adopted them, blending them into her very constitution, and founding upon them that inimitable system of Civil Jurisprudence, which has been the parent of our laws in Lower Canada.

In the reign of Louis XIV., surnamed the Great, those laws were re-written and with the revival of letters, arts and sciences throughout Europe, came the true revival of the Roman laws in all their perfection. It was under Constantine, a warrior of renown, that they were first codified; under Justinian, a warrior and monarch of undying fame, that they received their real life; under Charlemagne, also surnamed the Great, that they were partially revived, and under Louis the Great that they became permanently established. While Condé and Turenne fought the battles of the state, while Fénelon, Bourdaloup, Masillion and the soaring Eagle of Meaux-Bossuet, were pouring forth their imperishable floods of eloquence, when Corneille was reviving the Cid and Racine was tuning his harp to the pious ear of the nation, when poetry and eloquence, science and art were coming forth to dazzle the world, then the laws of ancient Rome began to resume their mighty dominion in the world. Dumoulin, Furgole, Domat, and others were stamping them upon the minds of the people. At the end of the seventeenth century, on the 9th January, 1699, in Orleans, there was born a child, destined to become one of the greatest writers of his age, one of the most famous jurists of all ages, that is Robert Joseph Pothier. From the year 1725 to 1772, the date of his death, Pothier wrote and studied and taught. He became an authority whose opinion is almost above question. His Customs of Paris, Customs of Orleans and powerful work on Civil laws bear the impress of a master hand, and his extraordinary treatise on Obligations, so often quoted in this Essay, served to establish most permanently in France these immutable principles drawn from the old Romans.

But have we lost sight of our text? What has become of *law 12*, which we were to follow the whole way down from the days of the Emperors? Open Pothier on Obligations, page 235, number 245, second paragraph, what do we find? "When any one has bound himself to pay two different sums of money under a disjunctive, the obligation is alternative and *he is only debtor for the smaller sum.*"

Here then, after one thousand years of burial, or rather wanderings through the mazes and ruins of barbaric devastation, we find our principle of the old *law* 12 renewed, or rather revived in the works of Pothier.

But if the laws were codified, and re-established under such great warriors and monarchs as Constantine, Justinian, Charlemagne and Louis XIV, you must necessarily look forward to some great monarch or great conqueror, who is to solidify them anew and to place them before modern Europe in a prominent and lasting form.

Such was reserved for the greatest warrior of all ages, this duty of law-giver to a people. Napoleon, having conquered a Marengo, having beheld "forty centuries look down" upon his victory, from the pyramids of the Nile, having seen the sun of Austerlitz gild the crimson field of Jena, and his eagles fly from spire to spire, until they perched on the towers of Notre Dame, having witnessed the Czar accept peace on a raft at Tilsit, and beheld Europe's kings feel for their crowns, and her emperors grope for their thrones, having become the patron of letters, the friend of David, the benefactor of Delisle, the admirer of England's Sir Humphrey Davy, the conquering Corsican prepared a monument that would perpetuate his memory and his name, long after the fading trophies of the Invalides shall be dust. He gave to France and the world the "Code Napoleon," the embodiment of the ancient laws of the Romans, with all their improvements and changes.

Let us look for the principle of our *law* 12. In article 1189 of the Code Napoléon we again find reproduced our principle.

Then upon this Code we find endless commentators. Aubry and Rau, Marcadé, Larombière, Demolombe, Mourlon, and a host of others too numerous to require mention here. From this Code and these authorities, our laws in Lower Canada were taken. By the treaty between France and England at the time of the conquest, Lower Canada received the guarantee that her laws would not be changed, that the French system would prevail, and it is therefore that our Civil Code is founded upon the French Code Napoléon, the authorities thereon, the works of Pothier and his cotemporaries, and finally, the great body of Roman laws.

Then our article 1093 reproduces the article 1189 of the Code Napoleon, which reproduces the number 245 of Pothier's comments, which reproduces the 12th law found in the body of laws given to the world in a new form by Justinian, which body of laws reproduces the laws derived from Trébatius, Labéon, Capito, Sabinus, Proculus, Julien, Africanus, Caius, Scœvola, Papinien, Paul, Ulpien, Aquila, and so on to the very days of the Roman Tarquins.

The reader may now form an idea of the immensity of matter presented to the real student of the law, the vastness of the fields that spread out for his exploration, and the endless horizons that ever widen before him as he goes. Also, he may judge of how important it is for each one to know something of the laws of his own country. It is not necessary to be able to trace them back to their spring or origin, but for the use of the present, in the actual affairs of life, it is obvious that he must succeed best and keep most within the range of the laws, who knows most about them.

It was with the object of conveying a few clear ideas upon this all important and fundamental title of obligations, that I composed and compiled this essay, and I only wish that my readers may obtain as much benefit from the perusal of these pages and find as much pleasure therein, as I have had in the penning of them. Trusting that this little seed may come forth, grow, spread abroad its branches and fructify, I cast it, at random, upon our Canadian soil.

INDEX.

	PAGE.
ABSOLUTE, when discharge of a debt is	85
ACCESSORY, Obligations are *principal* and	95, 96
ACQUISITION of property, modes of	14
ACTION AT LAW, when allowed	8
Of creditor is a personal one	30
When forbidden by law	46
Of debtors	86
ALTERNATIVE OBLIGATIONS: Those that are discharged by the debtor giving or doing one of the two things required.	70
Conjunctive	71
Disjunctive	71
ANCIENT LAW, defaults in the	56
AVOIDANCE of Contracts	35
BANKER not relievable for cause of lesion when contracting for the purposes of his business	27
BANKRUPTCY, definition of	69
BEGINNING OF THE CODE—1st Book	12
BIGOT—PRÉAMENEUS' opinions	71
BRITISH SUBJECT, definition of a	12
BY whom payment may be made	106
CASUAL, conditions that are	62
CATO's theory of penalty	97
CAUSES of Nullity of Contracts, Error, Fraud, Violence, Fear and Lesion	22
CIVIL and Criminal Actions, distinctions between and preference of	48, 49
CODE Napoleon on Conditions	66
Articles of our Code on joint and several Obligations	74-79
CO-HEIRS: How they are answerable to creditors	90

164 INDEX.

	PAGE.
COMMENTS, on joint and several Obligations	79
COMMENTATORS, on payment	102-108
COMMERCE, what are objects of	52
COMMERCIAL partners, law referring to	79
COMPENSATION, known as off-set, is the becoming of two parties, mutually creditor and debtor of each other	132
Code on	130
When may you oppose	132
What is necessary for	133
On what is based	133
Conditions for	134
Exceptions to	134
When optional	135
CONDITIONAL: Obligations are conditional when made to depend on any event future and uncertain.	61
CONDITIONS: There are three kinds, viz., Positive, Mixed and Casual	62
CONFUSION: The blending of the qualities of creditor and debtor in the same person	136
Code on	135
Frain's comments on	136
CONTRACTS: A contract is a convention whereby two parties reciprocally, or one of them only, promises and binds himself to give, to do, or not to do something	20
CONVENTIONS, definition of	20
CORPORATIONS: A Corporation is a body composed of one or many individuals, forming one legal being, and being perpetual, at least in theory	13
CORREI DEBENDI, what are	79
DAMAGES, explanation of	57-60
For non-performance of a contract	57
DEFAULT, explanation of	56
DELAY, damages caused by	59
DELEGATION, definition of	123
Concurrence of whom necessary for	123
Differs from Transfer: How?	124
Differs from Indication: How?	124

INDEX. 165

	PAGE.
DELEGATION—*Continued*.	
Differs from Novation: How?	124
Perfect defined	126
Imperfect defined	126
DEMAND, made on one co-debtor interrupts prescription as to the others	80
DEMOLOMBE, on joint and several Obligations	84
DEMANGEAT, on the same	84
DIVISIBLE and *Indivisible* Obligations: The former are those which have for their objects, things which in their delivery or performance are susceptible of division, either materially or intellectually. The latter are the contrary	87
EFFECTS of Contracts between third parties	31
Of Obligations	54
Of Payment	104
EMANCIPATION, definition of	13
ERROR, definition and explanation of	23
EXAMPLE of when an action at law is or is not allowed	8
Of Error in contracts	28-30
Of Effects, etc.	32
Of Stipulation	34
Of Reception of a thing not due	43
Of Offences and Quasi-Offences	47
Of Compound Interest	58, 59
Of Conditions	63
Of Failure	70
Of Bankruptcy	70
Of Divisible and indivisible Obligations	87
Of Payment	102
EXCEPTIONS: Which three can be opposed to divisible and indivisible Obligations?	85
EXPENSES of Payment: By whom borne?	103
EXTINCTION, of debtor's action	86
Of Obligations	100
FAILURE of condition and its effect	68
Definition of	64

INDEX.

	PAGE.
FIN *de non recevoir*, meaning of	96
FRAUD, definition and explanation of	25
FULFILMENT, of conditions and its effect	67
FUTURE, all conditions must be	62
GIFTS, *inter vivos*, meaning of	14
HEIR: The rights he has when sued on an indivisible Obligation	88
HISTORICAL, a note that is	114
IMPOSSIBLE, no one is held to the	53
IMPUTATION, by whom made and in what cases	115
Of Payment explained	116
INDIVISIBILITÉ *contractu*, meaning of	90
INTENTION, more important than the literal meaning	28
INTEREST, when law allows compound	60
INTERPRETATION of contracts	28
JOINT AND SEVERAL Obligations: As far as creditors go, give to each of them singly the right of exacting the performance of the whole Obligation and thereupon discharging the debtor, and as far as debtors go, bind the co-debtors all for the same thing, in such a manner that each of them singly may be compelled to the performance of the whole Obligation, and that the performance by one discharges the others towards the creditor	72-75
KEY-STONE of the Code is Obligations	16
KINDS of contracts	22
Of divisibility and indivisibility	93
Of Obligations: there are six:—1st. Conditional. 2nd. Termal. 3rd. Alternative. 4th. Joint and several. 5th. Divisible and indivisible. 6th. With a penal clause	61
LAW: It is a rule of action prescribed by a superior power (Blackstone)	2
As a source of Obligations	50-51
LAWYERS, a word to the	5
LAYMEN, remarks for the	7
LESION, explanation of	27

	PAGE.
MAP of Obligations	18
MASTERS, their rights over servants, etc.	46
MAXIMS taken from Roman law	22
McCORD, remarks on C. C. L. C. by Judge	10-11
MECHANICS, provisions respecting	27
MERCHANTS, provisions respecting	27
MINORITY and Majority defined	13
MINORS, when not relievable for lesion	27
MIXED conditions explained	62
MORAL, all conditions must be	62
MOURLON on penalty	98
NEGATIVE conditions, and what they are	67
NEGOTIORUM-GESTIO, definition of: A voluntary and personal act whereby one party binds himself towards another, in the management of his affairs, without the intervention of any contract between them	39-40
NOVATION: It is the substituting one debt for another, either by change of the object, by change of the debtor, or by change of the creditor	120-121
Opinions of Pothier and Duranton on	126
When there is a	120-121
Different modes of	124
Different kinds of	125
C. C. L. C. upon the question of	120-121
Commentators on	122
The will necessary for	123
Who cannot cause	124
NUMBER of articles under Obligations	17
OBJECT: *individuum contractu et obligatione*	91
Of this Essay explained	51
Of Obligations given	52
OBLIGATIONS: An Obligation is a legal tie by which one person is bound towards another to give, to do, or not to do something	19
When the law alone causes	50

INDEX.

	PAGE.
OFFENCES: An offence is the action of a person, capable of discerning right from wrong, and who by his fault, imprudence, neglect or want of skill causes a damage to another..	45-46
OMISSION is the failure in something ordered by law to be done	46
OWNERSHIP: It is the right of enjoyment and of disposing of things in the most absolute manner, provided that no use be made of them which is prohibited by law or by regulations.....................................	14
PACTE DE REMISE, meaning of the	85
PARENTS and their rights over children	46
PAULIENNE ACTION, when we may use the	36
What must be proven	36
And who may use it	36
Effects of the	37
PAYMENT, when made in fraud of the creditors—the consequences	35
When made before the term	69
C. C. L. C. on the subject of	103
Several examples of	108
Definition of	104
Is not only the delivery of a sum of money, but the performance of anything to which the parties are respectively obliged..	104
Who must make...	102
To whom we must make..............................	107
Effects of good or bad faith on.......................	104
PENDENTE CONDITIONE: Effects of fulfilment..............	67
PENAL CLAUSE: It is a secondary Obligation whereby the fulfilment of the principal Obligation is secured..........	94
PERFECT, joint and several Obligations that are.............	83
PERFORMANCE becoming impossible	137
The C. C. L. C. upon....................................	138
No one held to an impossible,.........................	139
PLAN of the Code..	10
POETRY in law, remarks upon the...........................	3

INDEX.

	PAGE.
POSITIVE conditions defined and explained	67
PRESUMPTIONS, when the law causes	82
PROOF, remarks on	140
The C. C. L. C. on the question of	140-144
PROPORTION, theory of penal	96
QUASI-CONTRACTS: It is defined under *negotiorum-gestio*	38
QUASI-OFFENCES: The same definition as offences, except that the offence is when the party is himself the actor, while the quasi-offence is when it is his servant, child, horse, or any one or anything under his care that does the deed	45, 46
RECEPTION: Obligations arising from the reception of a thing not due	42
RELATIONS of mandator and mandatary, contrasted with those of the master and administrator	40
RELATIVE discharge (express or tacit)	85
RELEASE, C. C. L. C. on the question of	127
It is the surrender, express or tacit, by a creditor of his right or claim upon a debtor	127
Real and *Personal* defined	128
Power to grant a	129
The effects of a	130
Code Napoleon on	130
RESUMÉ of error	23
Of alternative Obligations	71
Of joint and several Obligations	82
Of Subrogation	114
Of Novation	125
RIGHTS of payor and payee	103
ROMAN LAW on conditions	66
STIPULATE, no one can, for another	33
STUDENTS, a word for the	6
SUBROGATION, C. C. L. C. on	109, 110
Definition of	112
Pothier, Merlin and Grappe on	113
Systems of	112
Co-debtors in	81

	PAGE.
SUCCESSIONS : Future successions cannot be the objects of Obligations	14 and 53
SUSPENSION and extinction by term	69
SYNOPSIS of Obligations	145
TENDER and deposit explained	117
TERM, differs from a suspensive condition	68
Obligations with a	68
THINGS are movable and immovable	14
TRADERS, when not relievable for lesion	27
TUTORSHIP defined and explained	13
USE of a knowledge of law	8 and 161
USUFRUCT, *use, habitation, servitude, emphyteusis*, their place in the Code	14
VOLUNTARY administrators	41
WHOLE, distinction between *wholly* and	92
WILL, action of the	26

www.ingramcontent.com/pod-product-compliance
Lightning Source LLC
Chambersburg PA
CBHW032153160426
43197CB00008B/887